The Minister's Wife

The Minister's Wife

by

Huntly Gordon

(her youngest son)

ROUTLEDGE & KEGAN PAUL
London, Henley and Boston

First published in 1978
by Routledge & Kegan Paul Ltd
39 Store Street,
London WC1E 7DD,
Broadway House,
Newtown Road,
Henley-on-Thames,
Oxon RG9 1EN and
9 Park Street,
Boston, Mass. 02108, USA
Set in IBM Journal
by Hope Services, Grove, Wantage
and printed in Scotland by
Thomson Litho Ltd., East Kilbride

British Library Cataloguing in Publication Data

Gordon, Huntly
  The minister's wife.
  1. Gordon, E Olga M
  I. Title
  941.1081'092'4   CT828.G/   77-30624

  ISBN 0-7100-8846-9

Contents

Introduction

Mother died in her ninety-second year, tired but smiling.

She was a remarkable person, and had lived through the most profound changes in British history (1871–1963) without batting an eyelid. Orphaned in India in the days of the Raj and at first speaking only Hindustani, she was brought up in five successive English homes by the time she was ten. Such an experience today might well produce a juvenile delinquent whose unstable background, people would say, never gave her a chance. Yet when Mother had a home of her own it was as firmly established as if it were built on a rock; which in a sense it was.

She married in the face of family opposition, had three surviving children, was widowed at forty-eight, and spent the next forty-four years awaiting, with such patience as she could muster, the happy day when she could rejoin her beloved husband in a better world. But that did not prevent her from enjoying a very full life in this one. In fact her zest for life gave her a confidence that caused many of her friends no little anxiety.

For example, at forty-four, though her upbringing had excluded swimming and all other kinds of water sport, she thought canoeing would be fun; so, hiring one, she set out on her own into Cardigan Bay. At seventy-four she was found to be having secret motor-driving lessons to see whether she could achieve independence in road travel. At eighty, having travelled alone to Central Africa, 'because I had never been there before', she made her first venture into the air, hedge-hopping over the veldt in a small aeroplane from which she gazed fascinated at the herds of giraffe, zebra and ostrich stampeding before her. Her courage and eagerness for new experiences were boundless. And when, on entering her nineties, she reluctantly accepted the need to apply the brake, she continued to lead a life active in good deeds, in writing and painting, with an un-flagging interest in other people and world events.

By the time I was old enough to regard her as a person, and not merely as my universal provider, she was in her thirties; and from then on I speak with knowledge of fact, not fiction. Of her life before that time she told something in her memoirs written in old age for her family; and on these I have drawn, sometimes using her own words. Woman-like she had a life-long interest in pretty clothes, recalling many years later the details of what she wore on special occasions. In particular one may read her own account of how this artless Victorian miss won the man of her choice.

In Father's case the problem was altogether more diffi-cult, because so little of the material he left behind was suitable for my purpose. He had agreed to undertake the biography of an eminent Scottish 'divine', an exhausting project which took two years to complete. As a by-product of this work, he assembled notes for another book on the History of the Church of Scotland (not quite my subject), notes which were laconic in the extreme, merely jottings to prompt his memory. Unhappily illness intervened, and that book was never written.

Father was a shy man, with feelings too sensitive and emotions too deep to be freely committed to paper. Thus when, now fifty-five years after his death, I searched in his papers for some revealing details of what I knew to be a romantic meeting with Mother, a whirlwind courtship, and a marriage faintly reminiscent of Young Lochinvar's bride-snatching (another Gordon, by the way!), what do I get from Father?

On the way back we met Miss E. O. M. Constant (and my fate) at Lake Como in Italy, and we improved acquaintance at Geneva and travelled home together to England. We were married at St Mary Abbot's, Kensington, on 8th February 1893, and took our honeymoon trip to Mentone, Florence and Venice.

Such speed, I confess, leaves me a little breathless. Without doubt it involved Romance with a capital R. But you have to read between the lines of Mother's account to find it. And it has seemed to me better to leave Father's gaps alone than to try to fill them only from one's imagination. For to the understanding reader they may not be gaps at all; in fact, he may understand as well as or perhaps better than I.

It is to my great regret that I never got to know my Father really well. His legal, political and ecclesiastical upbringing and interests produced a gulf which was beyond hope of our bridging. He had his first stroke when I was fourteen and away at a boarding school, and communication with him in the holidays became progressively more difficult until he died seven years later. All I can say is that to a small boy he was a loving and tender-hearted Father; and on the only occasion when Mother insisted on his giving me a well-deserved skelping, he did it with a soft slipper and such obvious anguish that the very idea of repeating the offence (whatever it was) became for me quite unthinkable.

Of the depth of love between him and Mother there was never any doubt. She loved him during their twenty-seven years together, and went on loving him throughout forty-four years of widowhood; and in the end she rejoined him with a smile. One could write a book about them.

So I have.

1
Olga's Past

It has to be admitted that in Victorian times babies arrived, and often prematurely departed, in such numbers that the official record of these events was not always as reliable as one could wish. Especially was this so in India, with a regiment on the move in the hot season. Happily the entry we are concerned with is supported by a faded letter from Anna, the twenty-six-year-old wife of Major Frank Constant of the Bombay Army to Mary Anne, her seventy-year-old mother-in-law in Ramsgate. This gives the facts as we know them.

> Mhow Rajputana
> 11 May, 1871

My dear Mother-in-law,
A letter I received from Ellen [Anna's sister] a short time ago
tells me that you had a firm belief that I had left England in the
family way! Oddly enough you proved correct, though Frank and

I were quite in ignorance of the state of affairs; and I had been
led to believe that such a thing as having a child was most improb-
able.

A gentle smile must have spread over the old lady's
wrinkled face, framed in her long grey side-curls, and
crowned with a lace mob-cap and lappets. She knew the
early symptoms only too well, and the recollection prompted her to glance up proudly at her late husband's portrait
on the wall. Major John Constant was there immortalised
as a fierce-looking officer in the scarlet tunic and white
buckskin breeches in which he had played a distinguished,
and in her view decisive, part at Waterloo as Veterinary
Officer of the 5th Dragoon Guards. His plethoric and be-
whiskered countenance was turned to the left, as if impa-
tiently scanning the horizon for signs of Blücher's belated
reinforcements. In reality he had assumed this posture
on the insistence of the artist, who found his brush quiver-
ing uncontrollably whenever that ferocious eye was
turned in his direction.

To that same commanding gaze the old lady had ever
been readily responsive. And had she not in her time presented him with no less than twelve healthy offspring,
delivered — so he had observed — with the regularity if not
the speed of a modern Gatling gun? All of these had survived to adult life (four of them now doctors), an unusual
achievement which remained a standing tribute to her dear
husband's veterinary skill. Brushing a reminiscent tear
from her eye she resumed her reading of Anna's letter.

Fortunately things came off very suddenly. It came into the
world before its time, and I was quite unbelieving of what was
going to happen. I was taken ill at 2 a.m. on the morning of 2nd,
and Frank sent for the Regimental doctor. I was put under
chloroform and it was all over in three hours.

Won't you all laugh at my horror in having a little girl! It
seems a healthy but ugly little thing. We do not feel as if it really

belongs to us yet. Thank God I have been wonderfully well ever since. The child is being brought up on goat's milk, as I have nothing for it.

Fortunately we have been able to secure an English nurse, and a lady leaving the station had a lot of baby clothes to dispose of, so I was able to get some, for I had made no preparations of any sort for such an unwelcome visitor! I am being very strict as to regular hours and allow of no rocking to sleep in the arms. The result is we have no screaming at all and I dose it with homoeopathy. Frank is most amusing over it.

Forgive a longer letter but I am not allowed to sit up yet, as it is only a week since the birth.

A fortnight later another letter reached the old lady, this time from the proud father:

I doubt not ere this you will have heard the good news of Anna having presented me with a daughter. I can hardly believe I am a father, and Anna much less looks a mother at this time. However at our cost we know it, at times too well, for its wailing can be heard through the house. My work does not admit my noticing it much, though I feel it gradually growing on me, at times, to look on and amuse myself with its innocent and by no means ugly features.

As I do not approve of the idea of a black wet-nurse, I am having my daughter (bless her) brought up on goat's milk. As to names, I am going to have it thus: Emilie Olga Mary Anne Constant, your name forming a portion. What think you? As I have often told Anna, fortune (good) is ever with her. She sits beside me, looking as blooming as ever, and the infant sleeping in her cradle. We have had such a handsome present of mangoes sent us. They are Anna's delight.

But the Goddess Fortune, it seems, did not like being taken so much for granted, or spelt with a small f. And she could be vindictive. The next baby cost Anna her life. The child lingered fretfully for some weeks; then it, too, died.

As the Army was on the move, Major Frank had the little body sealed up in a box which had contained baby clothes sent out from England by his sister Eliza. He took it round with him until the regiment returned to Mhow, where 'Cyril Edmund Constant, aged 2 months' could be given Christian burial. Then he brought his little Emilie Olga Mary Anne back to England, and left her with Eliza and Sophy, his spinster sisters.

Soon he returned to his regiment, and after two years married again. Before long his second wife died in giving birth to a still-born child. Four years later Major Frank Constant himself died of heat-apoplexy in a train on the way home, and was buried at Lahore. At that point the Goddess relented, and closed the account. So a new life began for the sole survivor, our Mother, or 'little Olga' as she was then called.

Why Olga? Why not her first name, Emily? Both names were new to the family. Had there perhaps been some earlier Olga in Major Frank Constant's life? He was an unusually handsome man, and his father-in-law had written, 'I do not think I ever liked a man more upon such a short acquaintance.' Yet he did not marry until he was thirty-four. Did Olga then commemorate some earlier love? A Russian or Hungarian princess perhaps? The very name seems to carry a faint echo of bells, tambourines, castanets and other Balkan frou-frou. No? Well, that remains Frank's secret.

As to Emily (or Amelia), it was a popular English name in Victorian times, and possibly was Anna's suggestion. But Frank had simply said, as any Victorian head of a family would, 'I am going to have it thus.' No argument. Olga it must be; and so Mother was stuck with it.

When the Misses Constant, Eliza and Sophy, took on little Olga, they were in their middle thirties and lived in a small house at Tunbridge Wells. Their secluded lives were largely occupied in filling scrapbooks with newspaper cuttings which they considered would be of vital interest to posterity, and in running a Bible class. Though born as long ago as 1838–9, at the outset of Queen Victoria's reign, they lived so long that I myself (if I may be excused for appearing prematurely in this story) became aware of them in the early years of this century. I was then barely four and they were nearing seventy. Had it not been for the excessive amount of newspaper cutting imposed on them by the First World War they might have lived to be a hundred. As it was, they only survived into their nineties, to the disappointment of such relatives as admired antiquity for its own sake.

In my day Aunt Eliza was short and fat; Aunt Sophy tall and thin. Both were kind but formidable. They were nearly bald, spoke in gruff voices, had moustaches and scanty beards, and no soft curves anywhere. Both wore identical dresses of stiff purple taffeta, the upper part presenting a flattened breastplate surmounted by a whalebone-supported collar; in the unmentionable regions below, it narrowed to a sharp V and dived down into a voluminous skirt. A golden-framed cameo suspended from above on a black silk ribbon swung across this defensive corsage, tempting me sorely to let fly with one of my suction-headed arrows. When the Aunts walked, which was not often, their dresses made a loud rustling sound like a winter wind blowing through a beech hedge. I never felt we had much in common. Let us return to 1874.

Imagine then the impact of these Aunts on Olga, rising three; and, not less daunting, Olga's impact on them. She spoke nothing but Hindustani; for she had been left in the charge of a devoted Ayah and Bearer, who between them supplied much of the affection she needed. She now found that her chief entertainment was looking into a brass kaleidoscope and gazing at the endless variety of patterns that could be made by shaking together a few pieces of coloured glass. Yet somehow she felt that life must hold more than this.

Writing eighty years later, she said,

5

My aunts had to do the best they could with me when I arrived, but at first I would only submit to being bathed by my Father. Gradually I was taught English words and used to cause them some embarrassment on my walks in Tunbridge Wells when I would stop before a beggar and, pointing at him say: 'Dot's a jockaman (gentleman)', or to a gipsy flower-seller: 'Dot's a leddy'.

But the Aunts had their points. They played a cracking game of solitaire. For this, one was seated at a circular board of highly polished mahogany on which were some thirty little hollows, all but one occupied by glass marbles. The game consisted in making each marble jump over its neighbour into an adjoining empty hollow until the board was clear. One was expected to concentrate on this absorbing task in solitude, thus giving practical effect to their slogan, 'Children should be seen and not heard.' It was a game that tried the player's patience to the limit and beyond, in which event the marbles could conveniently be used as missiles.

The Aunts also ran a Sunday School attended by respectable local children. One of these in his later years captained Kent at cricket, which just goes to show. Olga didn't get around to playing cricket, but she began to learn her Bible, which soon had a growing influence on her life. It even began to pay off at an early age. One day Muscat grapes were being served at luncheon, and she was told she might have a few. Three were put on her plate; but she protested, 'That's not a few. A few is eight.' Asked to explain, she quoted the portion read at family prayers that morning which (I Peter 3: 20) referred to Noah's Ark, 'wherein few, that is, eight persons, were saved'. She got her eight grapes.

Whether it was that Olga suffered from an excess of 'solitaire', or became allergic to the sulphurous spa-water which was occasionally forced on her as a treat, she soon tired of Tunbridge Wells. The Aunts said they found her a handful, and altogether too much; so she was transferred to the home of her maternal Grandfather, William Fell.

Mr Fell lived in the Close of Lichfield Cathedral, where he occupied the position of Registrar of the Diocese and Probate Court; or on a more human level, that of poor Anna's father. Poor Anna's poor mother had died in 1854 (in childbirth, of course), and William Fell had later married Lydia Arden, daughter of the Rev. John Arden of Longcroft, Stafford. The Ardens claimed a clear descent from that Aelfurnie who was High Sheriff of County Warwick in A.D. 1080, so Lydia's family roots ran deep in English history. But not deep enough, for no sooner was little Olga installed in Lichfield Close than Lydia's roots shrivelled and she too joined her ancestors.

Mother recalls 'a faint recollection of the drawn blinds of the nursery windows which overlooked the South Door of the Cathedral and the Fell burial ground in the Close. Peeping round the blind I watched the funeral cortège intently in the hope of seeing Grandma's soul leave her body; but without success.'

Old Mr Fell, now finally widowed, became devoted to little Olga, and she to him. It was his quaint fancy that each Sunday morning his little princess should enter the Cathedral bearing a crimson velvet cushion before him. After all, he *was* the Diocesan Registrar; besides he found his pew uncomfortably hard. Olga slightly resented the publicity attending this menial task; but because she liked the cushion's royal colour and velvet touch, she humoured the old man. On occasion he did his best to supply a firm hand; and once, when she had been really naughty, he 'administered some (feeble) castigation in the nursery'. Olga trotted happily downstairs with him afterwards remarking, 'Grandpa, won't you have to use somefing harder next time?'

None the less the castigation taught her the value of a tactful approach. For, later on, when promoted to meals in the dining-room, she casually asked, 'Grandpa, what would you do if I spilt my bread and milk? Would you beat me?'

'Oh, no, my dear. I do not think I would actually beat you.'

Whereupon Olga pushed her plate away, and revealed a mess on the damask table-cloth.

'Look at that!' she exclaimed. 'Well now, what are you going to do?'

Well, what could he do?

Her days at Lichfield were happy ones. She had dogs, and a pony on which she loved to canter, with a groom in attendance. She made friends with the daughter of one of the Cathedral canons. They spent many happy hours together playing 'houses' under a spreading mulberry tree, which was lapped by the waters of the Minster Pool, whereon sailed a pair of swans.

But those days were too good to last. When she was about six her Grandfather became fatally ill. For a time Olga was still allowed to see him. She used to sit on his bed and sing his favourite hymn:

> I'm weary of straying, I'd fain be at rest
> In that far distant land of the pure and the blest,
> Where sin and temptation no longer appear,
> Where Death shall ne'er enter, nor sighing, nor tear.

But the time came when the singing had to stop, and to Olga's great sorrow she had to bid farewell to the old man. She loved him dearly for he had been more to her than father and mother. 'I was quite heart-broken,' she wrote. 'For days I wept and refused consolation, for he was everything to me.'

Her fourth home was with the Reverend Charles Cooper and his wife and six children in Birmingham. They were cousins of her mother's. Here she spent four happy years acquiring an education with a family whose religion was real and uninhibited. From a series of governesses she learnt to sew, to paint, and to play the piano and sing, which were the normal accomplishments of young ladies.

At first the six children were envious of her little coat and hat trimmed with fox fur, but soon she settled down as the seventh of the family.

With two of the girls she attended a missionary meeting where 'Mr. Charles Wilson gave an address about Africa, and he said that the negroes said we were very wasteful to eat butter but ought to smear it over our skins. As they had no butter, they had to use oil.' This rebuke sank in; so much so that in later years the two girls chose China for the scene of their missionary labours, where butter-smearing was not the fashion. And after a lifetime of devoted work among the inhabitants of that ancient civilisation, they narrowly escaped being murdered in anti-foreign riots because Russian agitators labelled them 'imperialist lackeys and running dogs'. As it was only too obvious that their running days were long past, they found the whole situation quite incomprehensible, and wisely decided to return home. Olga, however, was never involved in this, having had other ideas for her future.

From Birmingham the family moved to Aston, where there was a large garden that sloped down to the river, on which they had a boat. 'Uncle Charles,' she recalls, 'used to delight in rowing us into a small tunnel under a bridge, and shouting out our names. The deep echo, I was told, was the Devil naming us, and I used to scream to be taken away, *much to Uncle's amusement.* I also seem to remember terrifying dreams during that period and seeking refuge in other people's beds, *much as my children did in their young days.*'

These two passages (my italics) pose some thought-provoking questions. Why did this kindly Victorian clergyman delight in Olga's frightened screams? And why, when Olga grew up to be an Edwardian mother of children whose terrifying dreams made them seek refuge in her bed, did she not recall her own experience and look around to remove the cause? My own children were happily spared such terrors, and the continuing tendency

of their generation to seek refuge in other people's beds
has probably a simpler explanation.

The time had now come for Olga, aged nine, to be transferred to her fifth home. At the head of it was her uncle,
Dr George Constant, recently retired from the Indian
Medical Service, with a liver which gave a jaundiced tint to
the world around him. He had settled down in Tunbridge
Wells to be near his sisters, Eliza and Sophy, whom we
have already met. His retirement lasted some fifty years,
and in the absence of any other information it may reasonably be supposed that he spent much of that period
reading the books of newspaper cuttings which these ladies
had so painstakingly compiled.

On her arrival at her new home, Olga was brought into
Uncle George's dimly-lit study to be inspected. She found
herself facing a tall cadaverous man with grey hair and a
heavy white moustache, who gazed at her silently. Presently,
thinking to put her at her ease, the formidable figure remarked in a sepulchral voice, 'So this is the little thing
that kicked my shins in India!' Olga, unable to recall the
incident, maintained a guarded silence. She had hoped for
a little more warmth in his welcome. Yet she sensed it was
a welcome of a sort, and was grateful for it.

Uncle George had a wife and family. He had married a
sister of Olga's forgotten mother, a small strait-laced lady
with a bustle whom Olga was told to call 'Aunt Ellen'. In
spite of Uncle George's liver, Aunt Ellen had already produced seven children and did not really require an eighth.
But everyone seemed to think that Olga should now be
placed in a home where her dead father's brother and her
dead mother's sister could stand doubly firm *in loco
parentis*. And, as problems of relationship were often
settled by what other people thought, so it was decided.

On his Indian Medical pension and some private means
Uncle George was able to keep his family in reasonable
comfort (a cook and four or five maids living in, a gardener

and odd boy living out). One recoils from actually mention-
ing that ugly word, money, but there was no avoiding the
fact that Aunt Ellen's dowry had been on the meagre side;
and in a world in which social position depended so much
on one's 'means', this handicap continually rankled with
her. And when she found that a considerable sum had been
left in trust for little Olga until she was twenty-one, and
that Aunt Ellen herself could not touch a penny of it, the
unfairness of it all rankled worse than ever. The outcome
was that Aunt Ellen was satisfied that her feelings of
jealousy were justified, not of course for herself but for
her children, because their means — poor dears — would
always be so much less than Olga's means.

However let it be remembered to Aunt Ellen's credit
that although there was always a certain acidity in her
attitude to Olga, she never let it flare into a row; at least
not until they parted twelve years later. As for Olga, she
sadly missed the warm affection of her distant cousins, the
Coopers. But she put a brave face on it, and looked for
interests outside her Aunt's home. And when an incident
occurred which gave her Aunt an opportunity of getting
rid of her to a boarding school at Uncle George's expense,
Olga welcomed the freedom it brought.

A collecting box for soldiers and sailors, shaped like a
drum, used to stand on the hall table; and into it were put
small fines which Aunt Ellen levied from her children's
pocket-money as a punishment for minor misdeeds. One
day Montague, the eldest son, demonstrated to Olga that
it was possible to shake pennies out through the slit in
the drum. With these he was able to persuade their friend
the milkman secretly to bring in pennyworths of sweets,
which was against the rule. Olga was easily persuaded that
they were merely recovering what had been their own, and
for a while both shared the proceeds happily enough.

Retribution is apt to come in strange forms; and this
time it was as an earwig. Aunt Ellen, while arranging the
flowers on the hall table, saw the earwig and squashed it

with the drum. Unhappily in so doing she became aware
that the drum was much lighter than it should have been.
This led to a terrible scene. Accusation, prevarication, confession, disgrace; and finally confinement in their bedrooms
on a diet of bread and water as an example to the rest of
the children. Next day it had all blown over. But it hastened
Olga's departure to a boarding school in Tunbridge Wells,
run by an old married couple and their two elderly
daughters.

Olga recalls that at that school she 'was not very happy
at first, as they were great exponents of Fundamentalism
and the narrow Evangelical View'. Though the connection
may not be readily apparent, the children of this school
had to spend an hour every day lying on their backs on a
flat baize-covered board with a hollow for the head, and a
movable cross-piece to keep them in position. They also
had school prayer-meetings at which most of the girls were
expected to pray out loud. It was not enough to say with
the Anglicans that they had 'erred and strayed like lost
sheep'. They had to be specific. Missioners used to come
and address them, 'and harrow our young souls', thus
stimulating their sense of sin, and providing more material
for public confessions.

At this school Olga 'began to learn the discipline of
facing disappointments in a philosophic manner'. Too
often Aunt Ellen made plans to take her out on Saturday
afternoons; and she would wait patiently, all dressed up in
her best, only to receive a message that her Aunt's plans
had fallen through and there would be no outing that
weekend.

One of the chief activities of the pupils was collecting
for the British and Foreign Bible Society. They were each
given a little wooden box, shaped like a Testament, with a
slit at the top, with which they collected at home and even
in the street. Olga must have found the temptation terrific;
but she seems to have resisted it.

The curriculum at the school was centred on the Bible,

and Olga was an apt pupil, though certainly she never became unduly pious. By the age of twelve she was teaching a class of the smaller children at a Sunday School. It gave her a pleasant thrill to hear them greet her with 'Morning, Teacher', with always a curtsey from the little girls and a touch of the forelock from the boys.

Her departure from that school followed on the appointment of a new school barber. Olga had long fair silky hair of which she was quietly proud. But when the new barber had finished with it, it looked as if it had been savaged by a lawn-mower. She went in tears to Aunt Ellen. Aunt Ellen was small, but pugnacious. And when she realised that the issue was also between High Church Anglicans (herself) and Low Church Evangelicals (the school heads) her blood-pressure rose visibly. She went straight to the school and let fly with a fury that Olga found fascinating. But all she got in exchange was the repeated assurance that 'the hairdresser is a very godly man, and that is why we employ him'. This finally rendered her speechless, and Olga was removed forthwith.

Her next boarding school was at Notting Hill in West London, the Constant family having meanwhile moved from Tunbridge Wells to Wimbledon. Here she took her schooling more seriously, and Literature, French and German took the place of intensive religious instruction. She also had a piano in her bedroom, on which she was able to practise by the hour, refreshing herself from pots of home-made blackberry jam concealed in her wardrobe. When the girls were taken for outings they walked in 'crocodiles', two by two, and one of the Principals was always present to pair them off. If any girl was seen to be friendly with another, the combination was quickly broken up. Often it would be, 'Olga, you will walk with Mademoiselle (or Fraulein).' The proceedings must have closely resembled those in the exercise yard at Holloway, Ladies Department; but they were sometimes enlivened by Olga's talent for mimicry. This, though it appealed to the other girls, was less popular with the Headmistress, who was never quite quick enough to catch her.

For all that, and perhaps on account of her growing ability as a pianist, she was one of those chosen to attend the rehearsal in Westminster Abbey of the musical part of the service for Queen Victoria's Golden Jubilee in 1887; and next day she had a place in St James's Street watching the procession.

> The small widow in the landau drawn by cream-coloured horses was almost a disappointment, but one cannot forget the many handsome crowned heads who followed on horse-back, especially the beloved Emperor Frederick of Germany (the Kaiser's father) in his wonderful white and gold uniform; and also the Indian Potentates, resplendent in bejewelled turbans and gorgeous apparel, a great sight for those days.

Olga's piano-playing before long was judged good enough to justify special lessons from Mr Coenen, a teacher and composer eminent at the time. She went for lessons to his music-room in Soho Square, always chaperoned by her faithful friend Mary Crane, a maid in the Constant household. At a public concert she took part in a musical extravaganza by Coenen for eight pianos, played by no less than sixteen of his best pupils; real Hollywood stuff. She 'wore a very pretty pale mauve dress on a silk foundation, which rustled when I walked, to the envy of my companions'. It was her part to lead off with three bars of tremolo octaves, which each player followed in turn, giving a gradual crescendo before the main theme opened. By the time this happened Olga had tremolo-ed for no less than forty-eight bars; and, her initial nervousness quite gone, she hit her piano with a crash of relief to announce the main theme. The work received an enthusiastic encore.

There was in Wimbledon at that time a notable preacher, the Rev. Edgar Mold, whose services Olga loved to attend. Many were the verses marked in her Bible from which he had preached. One of his assistants 'roped me in to help her in weekly readings to a roomful of seamstresses at one of the big shops. For the first hour one read some interesting books, and then one read a passage from Scripture, making an appropriate commentary. It was rather a trying ordeal and I am afraid I did not keep it up for very long.' None the less she did it, and the seamstresses were too good-natured to object to this early form of Workers' Playtime.

When she was nineteen it was decided that she should come out at one of the Wimbledon Balls.

> I had a very pretty white tulle dress with wide skirt, long white kid gloves and all the necessary etceteras. However the strict religious views of Mr. Mold were more and more influencing me; and to him Dancing and Theatre-going were definitely of the Devil. My conscience seared me like a red-hot iron; and I felt I could not, as a professing Christian, go to this dance. So at the eleventh hour I abandoned my coming-out, and sent the dress to my favourite school-friend who could not afford such pretty things.

It was one thing for Mr Mold to disapprove of other people dancing; but, for a nineteen-year-old girl, longing to spread her wings, to sacrifice her own coming-out dance (etceteras and all) on a point of someone else's principle seemed to be going rather far. The Constant family must sometimes have wondered what kind of a cuckoo had grown up in their nest.

Perhaps Olga herself was wondering if she hadn't over-done it, for she consented to go with the family on their yearly visit to Drury Lane Pantomime. Unhappily, no sooner had they settled into the train at Wimbledon than they were joined by none other than Rev. Edgar Mold himself! (Moral: be sure your sin will find you out. Immoral thought: whither Mr Mold?)

> His shocked looks and words went deep, and at first rather spoilt

the performance for me. However the beauties of the final Trans-
formation Scene [the Pantomime was, appropriately, *Cinderella*],
which kept unfolding fresh vistas of colour and delight, and
fairies galore rising from opening flowers, was quite breath-taking
and made a picture long to remain in the minds of those who
were fortunate enough to be there. I do not think I suffered
morally from that vision of unfolding beauty.

It was a vision that helped her to a sounder assessment of
Rev. Edgar Mold, of whom no further mention is made.
Olga was growing up.

The next move of this restless family was from Wimbledon
to a house in Grassington Road, Eastbourne, where they
hoped to benefit from the sea air. Olga was by now within
a year of the time when her trust would be handed over,
and she would be financially independent. Already she had
an allowance, and with it she took the challenging step of
hiring a room in Junction Road as a private studio, where
she spent many happy hours playing the piano and painting. 'I painted on china, glass, canvas, wood, paper, satin
and georgette, chiefly copying little pictures or flowers on
sundry small articles which were in great demand for
bazaars.' The studio also gave her the opportunity of
engaging a little dressmaker who made several dresses
prettier and more fashionable than the grim uniform
favoured by Aunt Ellen.

The family always attended the Church of England
morning service at the Parish Church, as did most families
in the neighbourhood. Although they found the service
dull, it was a necessary social exercise, the hallmark of
respectability. In the evenings Olga also went by herself
to the Presbyterian Church. They always had good
preachers, some from Scotland, and the simple sincerity of
the extempore prayers appealed to her.

She also went away on visits to school friends. One of
them had an elder brother who not only made affectionate

advances to her, but after she left wrote her a proposal of marriage. As she did not care for the young man, she decided to be shocked at receiving his letter. 'I hardly dared confess it to my Guardian, Uncle George. When I did, I besought him to answer it for me; and I was not further troubled.'

Poor young man! I find it hard to dismiss him so curtly; for if things had gone differently he might have been my father. God knows, it is hard enough to be rejected by an attractive girl whom you lack the means to marry; but to get the brush-off in the form of a letter from a stuffy old guardian must have been bitterness indeed. I hope the sympathetic reader will therefore forgive a digression while we consider the sort of letter that put the lid on that young man's hopes.

Uncle George was by now a crusty sixty. It is fair to assume that when he learnt as a boy to write letters, his style would not have been very different from that of his brother Stephen. One of Stephen's letters now lies before me, written shortly before Christmas 1840. Stephen was no doubt anxious that his parents (John Constant the Waterloo veteran, and his Mary Anne) should be impressed by his efforts at school and in the right mood to greet him generously on his return; and he obviously took pains over his letter. The handwriting is in perfect copper-plate, clear and elegant. It would need a calligraphic artist to produce it nowadays. Yet Stephen was only thirteen. He wrote:

Leeds, December 16th, 1840

Dear Parents,

The approaching vacation, which will commence on the 23rd of December, and to which I am looking forward with great pleasure, reminds me of my duty of again informing you what studies have engaged my attention during the present half-year, and the improvement I have made in them. The subjoined will show you in what particular departments of study I have been engaged, and what progress I have made in each.

Studies	Began	Ended
Latin Grammar	Page 72	Page 101
Latin Exercises	" 40	" 54
Latin Delectus	" 4	" 15
English Grammar	" 71	" 85
Ancient History	" 1	" 71
Scripture History	" 1	" 17
Composition	Course 1st	Course 1st out
Geography	Europe and Asia out.*	

I trust that you will not only find that I am very well acquainted with such portions as are there marked, but also that my stock of general knowledge is considerably increased, and my habits of industry and order improved.

In conclusion allow me, my dear parents, to return my most heartfelt acknowledgements for the innumerable manifestations of your love and affection towards me, and I hope in return that I shall ever evince a desire above all things to please you, and to approve myself worthy of your love and esteem.

I am,

Dear Parents,

Your affectionate son,

Stephen Price Constant

Smooth work, from a thirteen-year-old! But the message which Uncle George conveyed to the poor young man had to be very different. Let us hope that even though his style retained some of the old-world pomposity of his youth his words will have spared the feelings of the defenceless lover.

I, being poor, have only my dreams;
I have spread my dreams under your feet;
Tread softly, because you tread on my dreams.

In the spring Olga went with Daisy, her eighteen-year-old

*The meaning is uncertain. Probably not the same as student slogans of today.

cousin, to Cambridge, where they stayed with the Bursar of Caius College. One of the students took her to a football match, where she thought the play rough and rather terrifying. At Evensong in King's College Chapel the singing was beautiful beyond words. Her experiences in Cambridge set her thinking of the wider world in which she longed to travel; so that she awaited with some impatience 2 May 1892, her twenty-first birthday, the day of her final emancipation. Relations with her aunt were by then becoming more strained.

> What made it more awkward was that, though being the eldest girl in the family, I was the daughter of my Uncle's younger brother, and so had no right to be addressed as 'Miss Constant'. It could not always be explained to strangers that this title applied only to my cousin Daisy; so I was often left out of invitations and made to feel the Cinderella.

When the great day came, and Olga at last had her own bank account, her first act was to write a cheque for £5 and give it to Mary Crane to do with as she liked. Mary posted it to her mother, the widow of a Wesleyan Minister, who not only was very badly off, but lived alone in Leeds. It was at a moment of dire distress, when the widow was on her knees in prayer, that the postman delivered the letter. 'So I was a proper Raven that day!' (See I Kings 17: 6.)

And that was not the only divine intervention at this time. A few days later Aunt Ellen announced that she was expecting her eighth child, and as Olga's presence in the house did not always make for peace, she had better go away for six months. 'My breath was almost knocked out of my body,' said she, adding with rather less than her usual tact, 'at the prospect of Aunt having another child at her age!' Olga however lost no time in arranging a trip with a school friend, Evelyn, to the Norwegian fjords at her own expense. She invited Uncle George to be their chaperone, an invitation which he accepted with alacrity. The bracing effect of the south-coast air on Uncle George had been amply proved and now he looked forward to a change of scenery. They all enjoyed themselves. 'We had a most delightful time, Evelyn and I each pairing off with a special boy-friend for the trip.' What Uncle George did is not mentioned.

Her next plan, already made, was for a tour of Switzerland and the Italian Lakes. On returning from Norway, she only stopped one day in London to collect a Miss Godberry, a middle-aged professional chaperone selected by Aunt Ellen; and next day they were off.

Olga's diary suggests that in her eagerness she had planned to see too much, too fast. Thus —

> Rather a rough crossing Dover to Calais, all ill in the cabin; got to Cologne very tired; shopped and went over Cathedral; wrote letters and retired early. Next morning to see Chapels and Treasury; 3 wise men, gold and precious stones and other relics; then to Church of St. Ursula, a visiting British Princess; walls and altars were lined with the bones and skulls of her 11,000 virgin attendants, who were slaughtered by Huns! Went to St. Peter's, saw Rubens' wonderful picture of Peter's crucifixion, upside down.

It was all rather hectic, not to say topsy-turvy.

For the next month Olga tirelessly explored the Rhine and its castles, Switzerland and the Italian Tyrol; cathedrals, monuments, pictures, waterfalls, hotel terraces, gardens, fruit markets and lake steamers, climbing up mountain paths, descending on cog-railways and diligences, amid gorgeous sunsets, and through rainstorms of tropical intensity. And all the time, tireless as the Hound of Heaven, Miss Godberry pursued her, 'And with unhurrying chase, and unperturbèd pace; and those strong feet that followed, followed after.' The awful thing was that Olga was paying her to do it. Once Olga met two Scottish clergymen who asked her to lunch. She accepted; but Miss Godberry, uninvited, insisted on joining them. After the meal the clergymen, rather than risk being stuck with Miss God-berry, excused themselves and made off without delay. Olga confided to her diary: 'Miss G really is a most sancti-monious person. I have endured it for a month, and cannot stand much more.'

A few days later came the laconic entry: 'Miss Godberry prevented me going to concert. Can't get on. Very hot. Went to church alone!' After church Olga wired to her cousin Charlotte, and Grace Brodie and her sister (school friends older than her), inviting them to come and have a holiday at her expense. And she notified Miss Godberry that as soon as this system of multiple-chaperonage was safely installed, her presence would no longer be necessary. Meanwhile they would press on for Grindelwald, Lauter-brunnen, Pontresina, St Moritz and over the Alpine passes to the Italian Lakes.

In her old age, Olga recalls:

In those days we had to do much of our travelling by Diligence. It was a hair-raising experience to have an outside corner seat on the buggy high up at the back of the coach, as the Swiss Jehu drove his six-in-hand violently down steep hills and round hair-pin bends over the wonderful St Gothard and other Passes. I have since gone the same way by motor-car, but that had nothing like the thrill of being perched up high and almost overhanging a precipice at each corner. The Swiss were excellent drivers and the horses sure-footed, and seldom was an accident reported.

Happily Olga's *Manual of Conversation* has survived the years. It is an early French publication for English tourists, suitable for almost any occasion. Here is an extract from the section on stage-coach travel:

Guard: Travellers are only allowed to take such luggage with them as causes no embarrassment. I see, Sir, that you have two trunks, a carpet-bag, a hat-box, a foot-wrapper, a cane, three or four parcels, a gun, a little dog and two Turkish pipes. Do you think we can take all that?

Traveller A: And why not?

Guard: Your passport is in order, of course?

Mr A: I have not one, and never have I been asked for one. The gendarmes have always let me pass freely.

Guard: I regret you cannot mount. Please return to the coach office. Here comes Mr Mastodonte, and there is but a single place left!

Mr M (at the coach-door): A little room for me, gentlemen, if you please.

Traveller B: What! a little room! Why, Sir, when people are as stout as you are, they should reserve at least two places.

Mr M: That is what I have done. Alas, they have kept for me one place inside and the other outside. Do you desire that I should be cut in half?

Guard: Would not one of these gentlemen be kind enough to take the outside place? That is the only way I see of surmounting the difficulty.

Mr B: Come! I will sacrifice myself for the good of the public. (The Guard helps Mr Mastodonte into the coach. The passengers exclaim:)

You are treading on my toes.

Don't sit on my knee.

Stoop! You are crushing my hat.

Ugh! You stifle me.

Mr. M: A thousand pardons, gentlemen; pray allow me just to get into my seat.

We had better cross our legs.

Stretch out your right leg.

Draw back your left arm.

Mr. M: Do I still incommode you?

Traveller C: Zounds! I am suffocated. Pray lower the window to give us a little air.

Traveller D: I have just put it up because the wind sits on this side. You must open the other.

A Lady (Outside): Sir, you have a place on the back seat of the coach. Could you be so kind as to let me have it?

Traveller E: With pleasure, madam. Do you feel unwell?

Lady: Yes, sir, I cannot ride backwards without feeling sick. I shall get better as soon as my back is no longer turned towards the horses.

(The passengers go to sleep one after the other. Mr Mastodonte leans on the shoulder of his neighbour who tries in vain to wake him up. All at once a loud cracking is heard.)

Mr C: Holloa! What is the matter?

Mr D: I think one of the fore-wheels is broken.

Mr C: Is there any danger?

Mr F: Danger! Stop, I implore you! Guard, pray stop the postilion!

Guard: Gentlemen, please to get out on this side of the coach. There is a wheel broken.

Mr F: Why, postilion, what have you done?

Postilion: It is not my fault. I was asleep on my horse. The coach has been against a post.

Guard: It is nothing gentlemen, a wheel and an axle broken, that's all. I will run to the nearest wheelwright's shop. In two or three hours we shall be off again.

Mr F: In three hours? Cursed postilion!

Mr M: Guard! help me to get out.

Guard: We shall make up for lost time. I will answer for it that we shall arrive at L tomorrow morning.

Mr M: Guard! Why don't you come when you are called?

Guard: I come! I come!

Mr M: Zounds! The accident could not have happened more opportunely. We are not above a hundred paces from an inn. Please to follow me!

So let us leave Olga for a while, enjoying the thrills of her outside corner seat, young, gay and independent; and look back to that other life-story which, unknown to both, was soon to be interwoven with her own.

2
Arthur's Past

Arthur's descent could be traced from Robert the Bruce, King of Scots, founder of Scotland's royal line.

That may sound quite impressive. But one cannot ignore the fact that seventeen generations had passed between them; and that during those five centuries, at the rate of two parents per person, Father also acquired over 130,000 other Scottish ancestors, many of whom must have been of less than royal descent. And of course, looking the other way through the telescope, the Bruce's blood, vastly diluted, must flow in the veins of the great majority of those who are of Scottish birth; not to mention quite a few who are not. So in the outcome, it seems 'we're all Jock Tamson's bairns'.

Ancestor-hunting can produce some rude surprises. But as Olga's roots go back unchallenged at least to Waterloo, one may fairly ask what was happening in our branch of the Gordons at about that time. Through the mists of the past, some gleams of light do still illuminate the scene.

In the wind-swept moorlands of Sutherland, beyond the salmon-pools and birches of Kildonan and some three miles south-west of Forsinard, lies a patch of green pasture with a Keeper's cottage and a rowan-tree beside the burn. To the north the open moor sweeps gracefully up to the summit of Ben Griam Beag, where a golden eagle has its eyrie. Southwards rise the slopes of Meall-a-Vorich, Hill of the Roaring (of the stags), from which in the evening the red deer still pick their way delicately down the deer-paths and gather like silent shadows round the house to crop the sweet grass.

It needs little imagination to sense other shadows there too, the shades of those Highlanders whose small crofts once clustered around Griamachary, the summer pasture. Here they spent their quiet lives in feudal loyalty to their chief, the Countess of Sutherland, and at her call sent many of their sons to fight in England's Napoleonic Wars.

In the early years of last century the Tacksman* of Griamachary, the head man of the village, was Adam Gordon, Father's great-grandfather. The Reverend Donald Sage, at that time Minister of Kildonan parish, has left a contemporary description of him: 'a shrewd worldly-wise man, with a throng family of sons and daughters. He and his wife (Besey Sutherland) lived in the exercise of the most unbounded hospitality, and at the same time economised so as to realise a good deal of money.'

Adam held his land direct from the Countess, having his own sub-tenants for whose well-being he bore a feudal responsibility. And that responsibility was a very real one, for during the long winter months Griamachary was usually cut off from outside supplies. As Sage recorded, 'Life there is bleak, bare and almost impossible.' Their shelter from the gales of winter was primitive. The walls of Adam's house, some 30 or 40 feet long and only 12

---

*Derived from tack, not taxes.

feet wide, were formed from undressed stones off the moor. Its roof was of turf and heather, weighted down with stones to withstand the tearing wind. Most of the surrounding hovels had turf walls only, roofed with wooden poles and heather. Peat was their fuel, stalled cattle their central heating.

Adam's dress was that of the old Highland gentleman: dark blue coat, knee breeches, shoes with silver buckles, a Highland blue bonnet, a gold-headed cane in his hand; and Sutherland gold at that. He spoke his native Gaelic, with English his second tongue.

Sage, whose preaching seems to have encouraged him in the use of superlatives, goes on to describe Adam and his (sometimes related) fellow-tacksmen in these terms:

> They were given to hospitality; were enlightened by divine truth and knew their bibles well; and to all comers and goers from the highest to the lowest could furnish a plentiful and hospitable table and lodging. But, as I shall soon show, this high-souled gentry, this noble and far descended peasantry, their country's pride, were set at nought and ultimately obliterated for a set of needy, greedy secular adventurers by the then representatives of the ancient Earls of Sutherland.

He was of course referring to the millionaire Englishman, George Leveson-Gauer, Marquess of Stafford, created Duke of Sutherland by William IV, who had married Elizabeth Countess of Sutherland, Chief of the clan. Unhappily the Countess was by then so anglicised as to be neglectful of her still loyal people. It had occurred to the Marquess, 'the Great Improver', that he might make more money out of sheep than out of Highlanders. His policy thenceforth was to drive out their people; and this was done systematically with threats and violence, and the pulling-down and burning of their homes.

The clearance of Upper Kildonan parish took place in 1819, four years after Waterloo, when the young men who might have resisted were overseas with the 93rd Sutherland Regiment. According to Sage,

> written notices were handed in at every house and hovel alike, for the Minister [Sage himself] , catechist or elder, tenant or sub-tenant, out-servant or cottar. But Adam Gordon had a life-rent of his farm, and those who had direct leases Sellar [the Factor] had no power to remove. The whole of Kildonan parish, with the exception of three families, nearly 2000 souls, were utterly rooted and burnt out. Many, especially the young and robust, left Scotland for ever; but the aged, the females and children, were obliged to stay and accept the wretched plots allocated to them on the seashore, and endeavour to learn fishing.

Adam did everything he could to prevent or at least to mitigate the heartlessness of the Duke and Duchess towards their clansmen; but to no avail.

Adam was by now sixty-nine, and Besey two years younger. They lived on at Griamachary amid the ashes of the surrounding homes for another twelve years. No doubt they were often visited by their sons returning from service overseas; for of their sons and grandsons no less than twelve were commissioned officers, three of them generals.

The picture reaches its most vivid and intimate with a tear-stained letter dated 23 February 1831 to Captain and Adjutant William Gordon in Aberdeen. Adam's day was done. Besey was nearly eighty when she wrote it, but her writing was clear and firm. The spelling is her own.

> My dear son,
>
> None that would wish me well would advise me to stope here after my dear Husband's death, for everything in this life is become a Desolation to me, and particularly this house where I have hade enjoyed such pleasure for many years past. It was your dear Father's requeast to me not to have anything more to do with Greamachary, and I tell you candidly that I am not going to remain here longer than Whitsunday; and had not my daughter,

Mey, agreed to stay with me untill that period, I would not stay a night. If you possibly can, you shall the first opportunity come to see me in my Dolfull state, and that may be the last sight I can expect of you.

Your dear Father's illness for the last five or six weeks was chiefly weakness and fainting. For the last month he was not out of the bedroom at all. In order to give him a little exercise a man would go under each arm to help him walk a little through the bedroom, but he would hardly gain one inch at every step. The last morning the last fainting proceeded, in which he expired as mild as a lamb. His memory, his hearing and superior judgment, with his bright faculties, was continued with him to the very end. He was not speechless above twenty minutes, regulated everything about the funeral and other affairs. The weather being very stormy give him a great deal of concern how the burial could be accomplished. But the Lord was visibly seen in the change that was brought about in the weather; although the people was warned in the hight of the storm, the day of the burial was amasingly fine.

The people of the Lord came forward, when they herd of his death, from the parishes of Leadern, Thurso and Reay, in all 116 men* was going down to Kildonan. Such a funeral I suppose was never seen in the North, everything done to the entire satisfaction of all friends and spectators.

Joseph got the coffin made at Reay by the best carpenter there, who accompanied the coffin all the way. 7 yards of velvet Black plate and cords was brought from Thurso; his name and age 82 years inscribed upon the coffin; a beautiful sight to everyone that saw it, price in all £4.

9 yeards of Cambric cotton at 1/10 per yd.	£	16. 6.
2 Ankers† of whisky		7. 0. 0.

---

*In Sutherland it was and is the custom that only menfolk attend a funeral. Many of them had struggled 30 miles or more through deep snow to Griama-chary. Adam's grandson Edward, then a law student, recorded that relays of mourners *carried* the coffin the 15 miles to Kildonan churchyard, through the same deep snow.
†17 gallons!

1 Bale of Oatmeal from Reay	1. 0. 0.
2 lbs Tea at 7/–, 1 Refine Loaf (sugar) 15 lbs at 1/3	1. 13. 0.
12 lbs Busquit	8. 0.
6 bots Port Wine at 3/–	18. 0.
20 quartern loaf of Bread	8. 0.
10 more pints of Whisky	2. 0. 0.
	£19. 0. 0.

The maner in which it was managed.

Such as came to Greamachary got tea, breakfast, everyone 3
drams* each. Such as met at Achentoul got 2 drams and bread
and cheese. The people who was only at breakfast got one dram.
The people meeting upon the road a dram as they meet. At Kildonan after the burial, the 116 men got two Drams each with a
piece of loaf, both high and low without distinction.

I send this with the inventory and valuation of your Father's
effects.

My love and kind regard to Mrs Gordon and the dear children.

I am, dear son, your Mother,

Besey Suthld Gordon

Inventory and Valuation of the effects of the late Adam Gordon,
Tacksman of Grimahery
10 March 1831

9 cows, as valued	£24. 15. 0.
2 horses	10. 0. 0.
24 sheep	6. 0. 0.
22 goats	3. 10. 0.
4 Beds	3. 5. 0.
8 blankets and pillows	2. 5. 0.
2 Candlesticks and snuffers	3. 6.
4 Fir chairs and 7 stools	16. 0.
5 Chests	1. 0. 0.
1 Looking glass	1. 0.
Mettle Crook	2. 6.

*A dram was about a third of a tumbler, at least on such an occasion.

1 Wash Pot and Bazen	1. 0.
6 cups and flats	2. 0.
2 Teapots and 1 Milk Pot	1. 4.
2 Tecanters	1. 2.
1 doz Tumblers	7. 0.
½ doz Dram glasses	4. 0.
½ doz egg cups	9.
7 egg spoons	7.
1 Saddle and sundries	19. 3.
New Testament and Psalm Book	3. 6.
10 Gin Bottles (empty)	1. 8.
	£36. 0. 3.

We, the undersigned, declare this to be the value of the above articles, according to our judgment.

Hugh McDonald, Cattle delar
Andrew Gordon, his mark X
Besey Gordon

The Inventory and Valuation tell us something of the frugal conditions of life at Griamachary. This family, well known for its 'most unbounded hospitality', owned household effects worth only £9. 15s. 3d. Think what they did *not* have! Surely the ancestral shade will not take amiss the suggestion that the last two items on the Inventory epitomise rather neatly the atmosphere in that happy home.

The careful reader may notice that whereas the valuation total is shown as £36. 0s. 3d. the individual items add up to £54. 0s. 3d. Tax avoidance? Unworthy thought! Perhaps someone's addition was a little erratic; as also with Besey's list of funeral expenses.

Soon after Adam's death Besey left home to live with her daughter at Reay on the coast, and before long the Griamachary house, like all the rest, crumbled into the moor. So much for the Kildonan Clearances of evil and unhappy memory. A wretched attempt to justify them, this time on moral grounds, is found in a report by Patrick

Sellar, the infamous Sutherland Factor: 'The People of Kildonan pay their rents by smuggling barley brought over the mountains from Caithness, returning the whisky to that county and Orkney, and by stealing sheep from the neighbouring farms.'

Today, on a great pedestal high on the summit of Ben Braggie and visible for miles around, there proudly stands a 30 foot statue of the Duke of Sutherland, waiting for the applause that never comes. His 'improvements' will long be remembered, but not in the way he intended. For it is his self-imposed fate to stand aloft there in all his loneliness, while the howling wind echoes in his ears the curses of vanished Highlanders. Stevenson wrote a fitting lament over that tragedy.

Home no more home to me, whither must I wander?
Hunger my driver, I go where I must.
Cold blows the winter wind over hill and heather;
Thick drives the rain, and my roof is in the dust.
Loved of wise men was the shade of my roof-tree.
The true word of welcome was spoken in the door —
Dear days of old, with faces in the firelight,
Kind folks of old, you come again no more.

Home was home then, my dear, full of kindly faces,
Home was home then, my dear, happy for the child.
Fire and the windows bright glittered on the moorland;
Song, tuneful song, built a palace in the wild.
Now, when the day dawns on the brow of the moorland,
Lone stands the house, and the chimney-stone is cold.
Lone let it stand, now the friends are all departed,
The kind hearts, the true hearts, that loved the place of old.

One could wish to have seen a picture of Old Adam. As it is we have a portrait of the eldest of his four soldier sons, Major John Gordon of the Queen's Regiment, who must have borne some resemblance to him. It is a fine face; the head erect, the nose straight, the mouth wide and firm with no sign of flabbiness. But it is the eyes that hold one's attention. Large, luminous, hazel, with a commanding but kindly look that invites trust and response. Yet the eyes of a disciplinarian, one whose permission his children must ask before sitting down in his presence.

Major John was invited by the Duke of Kent and Strathearn, Queen Victoria's father, to be his aide-de-camp, and he served in that capacity for nine years. When his son was born he asked the Duke if the boy might be named after him. 'Certainly,' was the reply, 'but be sure to call the young Highlander after my Scottish title.' So the baby was named Edward Strathearn Gordon, and the Duke stood godfather to him.

Major John's wife and son accompanied him on service to the West Indies, and three years later she died there of yellow fever. So Edward, aged three, was sent home to her unmarried sister in Inverness; and this admirable lady, Miss Jessie Smith, brought him up so well that the absence of parents proved little handicap to his development.

Young Edward's winning of the Gold Medal of Inverness Academy at the tender age of thirteen was the first public sign that he had something unusual to offer. At fourteen he entered Edinburgh University, was an M.A. at seventeen, and at twenty-one was called to the Scottish bar. He soon made his name in the successful conduct of cases for the defence.

One of these came to an unexpected ending. A bank cashier was charged with stealing bank-notes. The numbers of the missing notes were known, but they could not be traced. The accused man had a large family and was cast into the depths of despair at the charge. Mr Advocate Gordon took pity on him, became convinced of his innocence, and represented him at the trial, refusing to take any fee. His efforts were successful, and a verdict of 'not guilty' was returned.

That evening as the advocate sat before the fire in his

hotel room, glass in hand, savouring the satisfaction of having restored the poor man to his family, a visitor was announced. It was the man himself. Amid impassioned offerings of gratitude to Heaven and Mr Gordon, he drew from his pocket a fee of twenty pounds and pressed it on his deliverer; and touched by his effusive thanks the advocate finally agreed to accept it. But as he gathered up the notes from the table his eye caught sight of the serial numbers, which were fixed in his memory. Words, he afterwards said, entirely failed him; and he could do nothing but walk to the door and point the way out.

What a pity the sequel is not on record. The cashier, one supposes, resumed his job at the bank, thankful for his lucky escape. The advocate no doubt gave his fee to charity, and kept his mouth shut. But just how did he get rid of the notes, whose numbers, well-known to the police, had also been well reported in the papers? And, in so doing, was he perhaps an accessory after the fact? Only in later years, when presumably the cashier had passed beyond reach of the law, did he tell this story. Perhaps even in law sleeping dogs can sometimes be allowed to lie in peace.

Though his life's work was in the law, he shared the military tradition of his family, for he joined the Edinburgh City Volunteers and served with them for forty years, and on resigning he became their honorary colonel. Lord Chief Justice Cockburn, one of the greatest of Scottish judges, who knew him well, said of him, 'He is agreeable, modest and able, one of the very best specimens of our bar Celts. He is one of the few counsel who can be calm without feebleness and argumentative without vehemence. I predict he will rise high in his profession.' He did. Sheriff of Perth; Solicitor-General for Scotland; Lord Advocate, which in those days included the political responsibilities of Secretary for Scotland; and finally, Lord of Appeal, with a Life Peerage.

This Scottish lawyer certainly had something that

appealed to the ordinary citizen. In 1867 when he was to become Lord Advocate, he had to find a seat in the House of Commons; and the only vacant constituency was at Thetford in Norfolk. In those days Thetford had a population of 15,000, but only 210 of them were electors. Of these, 170 had already agreed to vote for the Whig candidate, Lord Frederick Fitzroy, who had been nominated and backed by his brother the Duke of Grafton. Gently but firmly it was explained to Mr Gordon that the result of the election was a foregone conclusion; yet undaunted the Scottish lawyer set out to canvass for votes. Within a week the local candidate retired, and the stranger was elected unopposed.

The reader will I hope forgive this possibly tiresome recital of Lord Gordon's virtues and achievements. Lightning only strikes in the same place once, and his descendants have since relapsed into a normal mediocrity better suited to the times we live in. But the position he won for himself forms part of the background for that other life story which, as I have said, was one day to be interwoven with Olga's.

Yet before we pass on there is one more incident worth recalling. In his last years the Lord of Appeal must have found his thoughts deserting the scarlet and ermine of the Bench in the House of Lords, and straying back to boyhood days beside the burn with his grandfather, Old Adam, at Griamachary. At any rate he approached the Duke of Sutherland with the request that he might be allowed to acquire the site of the old family home, so dear to him in his youth. He got this answer: 'It cost my people too much to get the Gordons out of the country for me to give facilities to bring them back again!' Once more words failed. . . . Later, Griamachary was among the deserted and unprofitable tracts of Sutherland which his Grace got rid of to yet another English proprietor, the Duke of Portland.

Lord Gordon's third son in a family of eight was born in

December 1854. It was a time when horrifying stories of the conditions of winter warfare in the Crimea were reaching the ears of the British public. Only two years previously the Great Duke had been laid to rest in St Paul's, and now it seemed that another Arthur Wellesley was urgently wanted. As no immediate successor appeared, some parents, hoping no doubt to encourage his reincarnation, christened their babies Arthur. But it was probably more as a tribute to the past than with any expectation of future military fame that the one we are concerned with was named Arthur Gordon.

He was brought up in Edinburgh, and went to school at the Academy. Though his class held no less than ninety-nine boys, their eagerness to learn overcame this disadvantage, and many of them were outstanding in their generation as soldiers, lawyers, doctors, professors and 'divines'. Yet our Arthur was no book-worm. He found time to play 'hailes with the clackan and a rubber ball'. At cricket he was a good round-arm bowler. He also played 'the gowf' on Bruntsfield Links using a leather ball stuffed with feathers and a couple of wooden clubs not unlike hockey-sticks; which perhaps accounted for his appalling tendency to slice in later years. His regular partner was his beloved brother Edward, or 'Diddy', one year older.

Arthur had light blue eyes, freckles, and fair hair with more than a gleam of copper in it. Owing to rough handling at birth his left eye could not turn outwards, so that he sometimes showed a slight squint; but his kindly expression and open smile made up for that. Following the Victorian fashion in Edinburgh, he and Diddy usually wore the Gordon kilt with horsehair sporran, green tweed jacket, and Eton collar with flowing red cravat. Both had their father's agreeable manner and engaging courtesy, and their habit of concentration was combined with a lively sense of fun. They were inseparable, known locally as 'the two robin red-breasts', and when the partnership was broken by Diddy's death from scarlet fever at the age of nine, Arthur was stricken to the heart. Even when we knew him years later he could not speak of his brother without tears coming into his eyes. And at the end this note was among his papers, 'Our comradeship remains with me as a clear and unmistakeable reality, and I doubt nothing of our certain future re-union.' Likely enough they are now together again on some celestial golf-course of springy seaside turf, with the larks singing in the joy of the morning.

When he was eighteen Arthur went to the House of Commons with his father, heard the great Mr Gladstone himself thundering in defence of the Establishment of the Church of England, and saw him deflated by the rapier-thrusts of Disraeli, their friend, the Leader of the Conservative Party. Fascinated, he decided that his future should be in politics. His father approved and he was apprenticed to a leading Edinburgh firm of Writers to the Signet. At the Speculative Society he met many whose names were to become well-known in Scotland. Among them was Robert Louis Stevenson, whose pale face, long greasy hair and velvet jacket were as unattractive to him as to the sedate citizens of the Scottish capital.

His father no doubt saw that Arthur needed a wider experience of life and humanity, for he persuaded him to spend a year in Suffolk in a newly established night-school. Here he taught reading and writing to 'great lumps of grown men', who were quite illiterate. As few showed the slightest desire for literacy, Arthur found this a depressing task; but he stuck to it for a year, and on the side learnt much about English country life. He also learnt to ride, and to milk cows. The children loved him.

Returning to Edinburgh to resume his law studies, he became his father's private secretary, and for three years had the opportunity of getting to know some of the eminent political figures of the day, Disraeli and Lord Derby among them.

Disraeli sometimes stayed with them when he visited Edinburgh; and Arthur kept the following letter to his father which must have appealed to him. 'My gentle friends' were, of course, his two sisters.

> Hughenden
> October 29, 1873

My dear Gordon,

You are the most trustworthy of friends, and are never wanting.

I have refused the Ath: and everything else but the real business. I can't say an address in a conservatory sounds very academic, and I think myself it is very infra dig: but it is too late to remonstrate, wh. I rarely do — only I could not stand having the dinner, wh. I think quite unnecessary, the day *before* the Installation. It ought to have been the day *after.*

You ask me what shall I do on Tuesday? Nothing, I hope, except see you, wh. is always a pleasure.

My kind remembrances to Mrs Gordon, and my gentle friends, whose slippers I am now wearing.

> Ever yours sinc.
> D.

Another letter which Arthur treasured was written on a small sheet, headed 'Windsor Castle', with black edging an inch wide. It was in the Queen's handwriting, and probably referred to a statement on the Scottish Reform Bill submitted to the Queen by his father through Mr Walpole.

> This is *quite* satisfactory,
> and the Queen thanks Mr Walpole
> for kindly sending her this account.
> Ap: 12 1867

During this period the Lord Advocate was much occupied in piloting through Parliament a Bill for the Abolition of Patronage, designed to ensure that parish Ministers in the Church of Scotland were appointed solely by congregational election, and no longer by the whim or influence of the local big-wig. This was a far-reaching change long sought by the Scottish people. The Lord Advocate's fervour on their behalf overcame Mr Gladstone's bitter opposition by a majority of 198, and the Bill became law. Mr Gladstone's comment to a friend was 'that bill of Gordon's was the cleverest move that I have known in the whole of my parliamentary life'. But there were many who thought that the High Church Liberal Leader had merely failed to recognise simple honesty when he saw it. However that may be, fervour and conscientiousness in Lord Gordon's case made a costly combination, for he worked himself to death in his middle sixties.

It was during the debates on the Patronage Bill that Arthur's sympathies became even more deeply centred on the Ministry of the Church than on politics. This was an inward process in the silence of the heart. The outward effect was that he resigned from his law firm, and entered Divinity Hall for a five-year course.

His notes, made some forty years later, tell in shorthand language some of his experiences during this probationary period: how nervous he was over his first public sermon, preached in the little Spey-side church of Kincardine that had heard thirteen centuries of preaching and whose usual congregation was by then only a round dozen; and his excitement afterwards as he watched ninety-four salmon netted from the dark Kinchurdy Pool nearby. He was at that time more at home on the river-bank than in the pulpit. As a small boy he had even taken part in a midnight salmon-spearing party with Colonel Farquharson of Invercauld at Braemar. The Prince of Wales had bet the Colonel that he would not succeed in involving the Lord Advocate in this illegal act; and the Colonel tried it on. The Lord Advocate's fourteen-year-old son, perceiving his father's dilemma, pleaded to be allowed to deputise for him. His father, relishing the opportunity to convey the gentle hint that salmon-poaching after dark may pass as a game for boys but cannot be shrugged off by men of reputation, readily approved his son's proposal on the understanding that the Lord Advocate himself was left out of it. It was a night that Arthur long remembered; torch-light flashing on the water, hoarse whispers, the thrust of the spear, Gaelic oaths, the convulsive kicking of the gleaming prize; all memories that would come flooding back at the prompting of the memoir note, 'Justice winked'.

In later years Arthur was to recall how as an assistant Minister at Blair Atholl he had ridden over the hills in a blinding snowstorm to take his first funeral; and been introduced to 'the uncle of the corpse'; and how the local laird, more partial to hospitality than to mourning, arrived with a hearty 'Well, Gentlemen, I hope you are all enjoying yourselves!'

Greenlaw, then Berwickshire's County Town, had been his first parish, to which he was elected by the congregation from a list of eight applicants. The church adjoined the Old Court-house, the vestry was part of the debtor's prison, and the Minister had to emerge through the iron-grilled doorway of the condemned cell. Hence the local saying:

> Here stands the Gospel, here the Law,
> And Hell's Hole a'tween the twa.

There were other late-in-life notes, of which one would have liked to know more:

For seven months I sojourned in the Castle Inn, awaiting repairs to the Manse, despite the old Church rule against 'harbouring in ale-houses'. Auld Jenny kept the toll-bar half a mile from the Manse. Parish Ministers on duty went free, but she had little enough, and I always paid her when I passed on horse-back.

My horse, and the night ride for Mr MacWatt to save the Beadle's wife.

Moscrip, the Carrier, dying. Why are country-folk so much more original than town-dwellers?

A reason for rejecting an application for a licence to preach: 'the aspirant has not always proved sufficiently *cautious* in the presence of strong liquor'!

I bicycle. [This laconic statement at that time probably denoted his first and last encounter with a 'penny-farthing', for normally he travelled on horseback or on foot.]

Comment from an old lady on hearing that a certain minister strongly disapproved of dancing: 'Hoots, the rascal! I ha'e danced with him often ma'sel'!

After six years in the border parish of Greenlaw, Arthur received a call to Kirknewton near Edinburgh; and three years later to the fashionable Edinburgh Church of St Andrew's in George Street. He hesitated before agreeing to follow so able a preacher as Dr John Stuart his predecessor, but was comforted by an old lady's two-edged remark, 'Don't you be afraid; St Andrew's people are very easily pleased!'

Again his notes include some oddities at St Andrew's. There was Miss Jane MacOstrich, who called and introduced herself as the Holy Ghost, and, the door being closed on her, was heard to exclaim: 'Damned Fool!'; the woman far gone in elephantiasis, and her visitor who asked, 'Why don't you go to Church?'; the Russian lawyer who had performed the feat of marrying two wives, each with a wooden leg; and the perplexed minister from Cape Wrath, whose fishermen parishioners attributed their lethargy in church-going to the inactivity of the Holy Ghost among them.

After two years of this exacting Edinburgh parish, Arthur began to suffer from stress and sleeplessness. He was persuaded to go for a holiday to Palestine with Huntly, his youngest brother, now a lawyer in Edinburgh. On that trip he met some strange and interesting people — among them Stanley, the African explorer, who told him that he had spent the night before his marriage lying on the floor of Westminster Abbey with a bad attack of

African fever, and only struggled through next day's ceremony with a heavy dose of opiates. These he strongly recommended for sleeplessness.

Then there was the American Methodist Bishop who expected to find in Damascus the 'bulls' which Layard had discovered at Nineveh; and who was urging his exhausted party on their way with frequent reminders of the number of dollars each hour in Europe was costing them. There was the fat lady who on reaching the goal of her pilgrimage, the Well of Jacob, merely complained that the water was 'nasty'. There was Mrs X from California who was on her way to Edinburgh for surgical attention, proudly proclaiming her record: 'I must be the first of my country-women to have been operated on for cancer in five capitals of Europe!'

Their visit to the Holy Places in Jerusalem was deeply impressive in spite of the crowds. From Calvary they went to the Church of the Holy Sepulchre, the very place of the Resurrection. Arthur, trying to visualise the scene, raised his eyes to heaven, only to find himself gazing into the features of a well-known Edinburgh insurance manager, who thoughtfully reminded him that his life policy was due for renewal.

From Palestine they went by sea to Egypt, a journey on which Cook's agent was surprised at Arthur's 'remarkable powers of sea-sickness'. In their brief visit to Egypt it was typically the people rather than the sights that interested them. They had an introduction to Sheik Morgani, a leading land (and slave) owner in the Sudan who had sided with Britain in the campaign against the Mahdi. He had gone to London for the Queen's Jubilee in 1887, and visited her at the Palace. When the Duke of Connaught presented him, the Queen, remembering that to kiss the hand of a woman might be contrary to custom for a descendant of Mohammed, greeted him with a cordial handshake. Such royal consideration made the Sheik her devoted admirer for life, and a friend to British visitors to Egypt.

It was barely an hour before midnight when, at the invitation of Sheik Morgani, the Gordon brothers drove through the grounds of his beautiful Palace among the palm-trees. Howling dervishes disported themselves in the torch-lit gardens around the courtyard. The Sheik received his guests in a spacious hall adorned with ancient and precious tilework, where a few guests were already seated on divans. He was a genial and charming man, a perfect host whose English they could understand without difficulty. After some conversation he passed them on to another guest, a magnificently dressed Sheik, Zobair Pasha by name. It so happened that Arthur knew Zobair to be one of the most powerful figures in the Sudan, and one who had been hand-in-glove with the Mahdi. His son, after repeated warnings, had been executed by General Gordon for slave-trading. The General's subsequent murder by the Mahdi's soldiery at Khartoum had no doubt gone some way to satisfy Zobair's longing to avenge his son's execution; but Arthur must have felt at that moment that it would be tactless to give unnecessary prominence to the name of Gordon.

Zobair drank coffee with them, exchanging courtesies through his interpreter. He presently made the graceful gesture between head and heart which implied that they were accepted as his personal friends. He next asked their names. 'Gordon.' There was an uneasy pause. Zobair's hand moved quietly to the jewelled hilt of his dagger, and a hard look came into his eyes. 'Are you then members of General Gordon's family?' Not his immediate family, was the reply, but his tribe or clan. Arthur then calmly turned the conversation to the subject of crocodiles on the Nile. Somewhat to their relief Zobair relaxed and responded with a story which, as it proceeded, developed into a parable.

'I will tell you', he said, 'of a fight I once saw between a Crocodile and a Lion far up the Cataracts. The Crocodile was on shore some distance from the river, and the Lion was between him and the water, crouching ready to spring. The Crocodile, raising himself on hind legs and tail, awaited the Lion's attack. When he could hold his position no longer, he came down, and started to make for the river. At that instant the Lion sprang over the threatening jaws and with one stroke of its paw broke the Crocodile's neck.' And for good measure the Pasha added with some emphasis, 'I have in my day killed many crocodiles, many lions, many elephants. I have also slain many *men*.' This aptitude for promiscuous slaughter more than confirmed their suspicion that his story really described Kitchener's victory at Omdurman, the breaking of the Mahdi's power, and the avenging of General Gordon's death. However that may be, the brothers breathed more freely when their blood-thirsty host brought the interview to a peaceful conclusion.

Back in Edinburgh Arthur's sermons at St Andrew's and his talks with his parishioners gained fresh interest from his travels in Palestine.

In 1892 Arthur was commissioned by the General Assembly of the Church of Scotland to visit the Waldensian Church together with his friend Richard Brown, a chartered accountant and Elder of the Kirk. Did you say what and where is this Waldensian Church? Well, I didn't know either.

In 1170 Peter Waldo, a rich merchant of Lyons, sold all his goods and gave the proceeds to the poor. His followers, the Waldenses, preached the simple teaching of Christ, whereas the Franciscans emphasised the person of Christ. For this deviation from the official Roman Catholic line, Waldo was excommunicated by the Pope in 1184, and his followers took refuge in the hills and valleys of north-west Italy.

In 1655 an army of French troops and of Irish soldiers who had fled from Cromwell entered these valleys and in the name of the Pope massacred the Waldenses with the utmost barbarity. Cromwell called on the Protestant powers to join England in a remonstrance to the French King; and Milton helped by writing his famous sonnet 'On the late Massacher in Piemont':

Avenge, O Lord, thy slaughter'd Saints, whose bones
Lie scatter'd on the Alpine mountains cold.

Large sums of money were collected in England and sent to the Waldenses to relieve their sufferings and enable this branch of the Protestant movement to withstand the power of the Vatican. And, ever since then, the Protestant Churches in Scotland and elsewhere have maintained a sympathetic contact with the Waldenses.

For about a fortnight Arthur and Richard Brown, as delegates from Scotland, travelled among the remote Alpine villages where these early Protestants had taken refuge. For them it was like an excursion into the past of their own country; as though they were among the Scottish Covenanters in the bloody days of the seventeenth century, when Protestants were driven to hold their services secretly among the heathery rocks and hidden recesses of the mountains, with look-outs posted to give warning of their persecutors. And there were the same stories of brutality and murder for those who held to their faith. Though the people were poor, the Scottish visitors were greeted with true hospitality; and when they left they took with them the warm greetings and thanks of the Waldensian Church to their Scottish supporters.

Much refreshed in body and mind from their interesting and congenial visit, Arthur and Richard made their leisurely way home by train through Turin and Milan, and north to the Italian Lakes. Charmed by the scenery they stopped off at Como, and took a steamer trip up the lake to Menaggio. Tomorrow, they said, they would go overland to Lake Lugano.

The warmth and sunshine, the colourful dresses and the

gay carefree Italian way of life contrasted strongly with the stern call of work in the grey northern capital to which they were returning. Outwardly at least there was no complaint about that. But if duty was to be the only call, might not life become rather a narrow affair? Were they by any chance missing something? That night a flaming sunset cast its romantic spell, and set their thoughts a-wandering in the world of the might-have-been, and even perhaps of the might-yet-be. There, briefly, let us leave them.

Earlier I referred to the little Spey-side church in which Arthur preached his first sermon. It would seem fitting here to tell of a local legend concerning Kincardine Church.

This small white-washed building, standing alone in the fields mid-way between Aviemore and Nethybridge, might be mistaken for an ordinary farm-house were it not for the stone belfry at one end. From this, once a month, the bell rings out calling together the small remnant of a once populous parish who keep alive the unbroken tradition of more than thirteen centuries of Christian worship at this spot.

There is a local legend that the site of the church was previously a fairy-knoll; and that the three Spey-side churches of Insh, Alvie and Kincardine were founded by missionaries sent out by St Columba from Iona in the sixth century. The foundations of the present building at Kincardine are of the twelfth century or earlier; and the Leper's Blink, through which the celebration of High Mass could be watched from outside, dates the existing walls to a time before the Reformation of 1560. Even within its known history the church has survived some stirring events. Towards the end of the fifteenth century a raiding party of Cummings, closely pursued by their enemies, took refuge in it. A burning arrow set the thatched roof alight, and all those who tried to escape from the fire were cut down by the sword. Of the history of local events in the eight previous centuries nothing survives.

A gentler story of the fifteenth century recalls that the fifth Baron of Kincardine married a daughter of Cameron of Locheil. On her death-bed she asked to be buried in the soil of her beloved Lochaber, and soil from her home was brought here for the purpose. The earth evidently contained the seeds of Sweet Cicely (*Myrrhis odorata*) which grows nowhere else in the Kincardine district. And now, five centuries later, some clumps of it continue to flourish near the church, where it is still known as 'The Baron's Lady's Flower'.

Immediately outside the church door is a large granite block, deeply sunk into the ground. Its oval top is hollowed, but has no drain-hole or overflow. The stone may perhaps have been used as a font or for Holy Water; and for that reason was dragged out of the church at the Reformation. But the absence of any carving, however crude, raises the possibility that it retained its ceremonial importance from pre-Christian times, when perhaps it may have been a sacrificial altar-stone. Near it lies a rusty iron framework which, when bolted round a coffin, was no doubt a good form of insurance against the body-snatchers of the last century.

Internally there have been few changes since early Victorian times; some pallid stained glass, and more happily a modern pulpit and Communion Table. But there still remain the rigour of the pews, the brass oil-lamps, the massive coke stove, and the 'ladle' for taking the collection. This uncompromising wooden box on its four-foot long handle can suddenly appear under your nose; so it is well to have your money ready if you want to avoid embarrassment.

Nowadays we sing with a harmonium. But when Father took his Beginners' Service here a hundred years ago, a Precentor with a tuning-fork led the congregation through the praise. No doubt they sang at least as well then as now. Today that same Precentor's son in his old age lives alone in his father's croft high on an Abernethy hillside. He is known all around as 'the Fiddler', for he too has music in his soul.

3
The Nuptial Dance

For young ladies the Victorian system of chaperonage no doubt served a useful, even an essential purpose. Performed by a lady of discretion, it kept undesirable persons at a safe distance, while allowing acceptable persons seemly access to the object of their affections; at least until the whole situation got out of control. Unhappily Miss Godberry, Aunt Ellen's choice for a chaperone, was not a lady of discretion. She was an embittered spinster who regarded it as her mission for the time being to see that Olga had no fun at all. But now her time was up. Reinforcements arrived from England in the shape of Cousin Charlotte Fell and the two Brodie sisters, all of them Olga's seniors but not too rigorous as guardians; and Miss Godberry, inwardly fuming at her dismissal and bilious from the jolting of excessive coach-travel, returned to England.

After a week of delightful excursions and watercolour sketching around Lake Como, the four ladies decided to return home by easy stages. They took the steamer across to Menaggio whence a quaint little tram-train would take them overland to Porlezza on Lake Lugano. But let Olga tell her innocent story in her own way:

'Though I had booked first class throughout by Cooks, I naturally travelled with the other three who had only taken second class tickets; and we therefore had to carry our own luggage. I struggled along the platform in the wake of the others with a heavy bundle of wraps in one hand and a most plebeian basket-hamper in lieu of a hat-box in the other. I was just preparing to follow my friends into an over-crowded compartment, when I heard a courteous Scottish voice saying: "I think you will find more room in here." and hands were stretched out to relieve me of my burdens.

'Having been brought up in strict chaperonage style, I was somewhat perturbed to find that the only occupants of this first class carriage were two gentlemen in tweeds, evidently friends. However I sat demurely in the corner farthest away from them. Before we started the ticket collector came round and I had to pass my ticket-book across; which opened up a conversation with one of the kindly travellers, the one with the deer-stalker hat, a cropped auburn moustache and smiling eyes, who had first spoken to me.'

[And what, it may be asked, were Arthur's impressions of his new travelling companion? From the train window he had watched her struggle along the platform, laden with luggage. Something had prompted him daringly to call out to her; and he had been secretly thrilled when, after a brief glance, she came trustfully towards him. And there she now sat, prettily flushed, a little embarrassed at finding herself alone with two strange men.

Her tailored jacket and voluminous skirt could not altogether disguise her neat and shapely figure. From her light-brown hair, drawn severely back as fashion demanded, an untidy tendril had escaped, and hung down in joyful abandon. She wore a jaunty little green hat with a light brown feather. As she looked shyly across at Arthur and smiled, he noticed that her hazel-brown eyes had flecks of green light in them that harmonised very attractively with the colours in her hat. He also realised with a slight start that it was not usual for him to be observing the colours in a young lady's eyes.] Olga continues:

'About that time there was a scare of cholera in Paris, and we naturally discussed alternative ways home. I remember that my new acquaintance impressed on me that, whatever I decided, Cook's Office at Geneva would be the best place at which to change my tickets.

'On reaching the rail terminus at Porlezza, my new friends kindly brought my hand-luggage on to the steamer, and I went forward to rejoin Charlotte and the Brodies so that I should not appear to be travelling alone and unguarded. But both my rail companions followed and were not inclined to quit, and I had the impression that Cupid's Dart had perhaps pierced two hearts!

'On the lake we crossed the Swiss frontier, and while the Customs men examined the luggage, I remained in the bows having a most interesting conversation with one of my new friends. He and his companion were returning from a visit to the Waldensians. He told me of their story, so like that of the Israelites of old, and mentioned an excellent book on the subject which he thought I might like to read. In order that I should not forget the title and author, he took out his card-case, and wrote it on the back of his card which he gave me. I put it into my purse without further examination.

'Arriving at the Lugano jetty I once more seized my portables and, bowing to my two travelling companions, walked sedately off the boat flanked on either side by the Brodies and followed by Cousin Charlotte, without anything in the way of a backward glance. On reaching the privacy of my hotel bedroom, my first act was to look at the visiting card, on which I found: "Rev. Arthur Gordon, St Andrew's, Edinburgh." Was this the answer to one of my dreams? I prayed that at least we might meet again.

'That evening I had a severe lecture from Charlotte and the elder Brodie sister on talking to strange men. But I said I had no alternative, and our conversation was only innocent and interesting.

'The following day the Brodie sisters had to leave for England; and Cousin Charlotte and I spent a few days at Lugano before going on to Baveno on Lake Maggiore where we did some more painting. My surprise was great, on the day after our arrival there, to receive a letter, signed by Arthur Gordon, telling me the places and hotels where he and his friend would be staying, with dates. It seems that on the little train-journey I must have mentioned — en passant! — some of the places we would be visiting; and Mr Gordon's memory must have been very retentive. I think I answered his letter saying where we might be, with dates, but certainly was not so brazen as to mention our hotels. I did not bother to tell all this to Cousin Charlotte.

'Eventually, taking the stage-coach over the Simplon Pass and down the Rhône Valley, we reached Geneva after a journey of nearly 200 miles. Next day Charlotte had one of her headaches and remained in her hotel room, while I spent long hours sitting on Rousseau's Island which overlooked the main bridge, wondering if I might again catch a sight of my two fellow-travellers. But alas! My hopes were disappointed.

'Next day Cousin Charlotte and I called at Cook's to alter our homeward route to avoid Paris because of the cholera scare. When I handed over my cheque for the extra fare, the Assistant looked at it and said, "A gentleman was here earlier, Miss Constant, asking for your hotel address." It was a moment of some embarrassment.

'Next morning, Sunday, I came down early to breakfast at the Hôtel des Bergues and, as I sat alone at my table for two — for Charlotte was having rolls and coffee in her bedroom — I saw in a far corner a clergyman who seemed rather like the friend in tweeds whom I had met on the train at Menaggio; and I did not get very far with my breakfast!

'As I left the restaurant, I was followed out by the Padre, and there coming down the stairs was his friend. Presently Charlotte came down. She raised her eyebrows on seeing me in conversation with two men; but I introduced her, reminding her how very kind they had been in helping with our luggage on the Lake Lugano steamer. Before long Charlotte began to thaw, and later we all went off to service in the English Church.

'In the afternoon we four went for a short outing on the Lake of Geneva; and in the evening I remember having a long talk with Mr Gordon about his visit to Palestine, and his seeing "Gordon's Calvary", the site favoured as authentic by General Gordon; and the Garden Tomb. He offered to send me photographs of both; and so I had to give him my home address!

'I also had to explain that I lived with an Aunt and Uncle and their family at Eastbourne, my parents having died when I was young; and as two brothers had married two sisters, any letter addressed to Miss Constant would of course be given to their daughter, Daisy; so it was essential that my Christian name, Olga, be put on my letters.

'By a happy coincidence Mr Gordon and his friend Mr Richard Brown were due to leave Geneva for England by the very same train on which my cousin and I had booked seats. We therefore arranged to have a compartment together, as Britishers. We got to Victoria about 6.30 p.m., and as we both went our separate ways, Mr Gordon bade me farewell saying, "I do hope we may have the pleasure of meeting again." Till that moment I had never met a man of such courtesy and graciousness. Their number is rare.

'As Cousin Charlotte and I sped south to Eastbourne my heart was in the depths. I was returning to conditions far from congenial, and would never be likely to travel to the North, and that might be the end of Love's Young Dream!

'The centre of interest at home was of course Aunt Ellen's baby, then ten days old. Aunt Ellen was quite coy over him; and when he was baptised later, I was one of his godmothers.

'I kept fairly quiet about my recent experiences, and so did Cousin Charlotte. But not long after our return, to my amazement, a large wooden case arrived for me containing two large photographs, as he promised. I explained this to Aunt Ellen as casually as I could. Then, a few days later, came a letter most carefully addressed to "Miss Olga Constant". It contained an offer of marriage. I was flabbergasted!

'In those days it was de rigueur that "suitors" first applied to the parents before proposing. In my case, however, Mr Gordon knew nothing of my circumstances or relations. But he had evidently written to Cousin Charlotte giving particulars of his family and his work and his intentions towards me, which was all he could do. Charlotte and her mother had replied by inviting Mr Gordon to stay with them in Eastbourne; and she told me this when I told her of the important letter.

'So I wrote back in a non-committal way saying I could not give a definite answer till I had spoken to my Guardians; and their attitude I was afraid would be obstructive. However I indicated at the same time that, for my part, the answer might be not unfavourable.

'Charlotte was a brick about it. She promised to see Aunt Ellen, to describe the position and give her view of Mr Gordon. That was on the Friday, while I spent the afternoon with other friends in Eastbourne. On my return, Aunt Ellen said nothing; nor on Saturday. Only after a tête-à-tête tea on the Sunday did my Aunt open up the question. I am afraid I can neither forget nor forgive her tone when she said, "Who *is* this Mr Gordon? Surely you cannot intend to marry him? But he is a *Presbyterian*!"

This last as an expression of utter contempt. I stuck to my guns, and replied "Yes" to everything; and reminded her that I was accustomed to attending the Presbyterian Church every Sunday evening.

'After dinner it was Uncle George's turn to have a go. His main point was the disparity in our ages, I being 21½ and Mr Gordon 37, which made it a very unsuitable match; but when I reminded him that there was the same difference in ages between him and Aunt Ellen, the argument lost much of its force. Then it was insinuated that I was being married for my money, a subject of which Mr Gordon knew nothing; indeed as I had been travelling mostly second class, he might well have thought I had very little money. Besides his letter had said he had enough means of his own to support a wife in quiet comfort.

'In due course Mr Gordon arrived in Eastbourne, and called on Dr and Mrs Constant. I heard, but did not see his arrival. At last I was summoned to meet my future husband in the presence of the whole family. Could anything be more harsh and tactless for a young and rather emotional girl than such an ordeal! But I entered dressed for a walk to Beachy Head, and so before long we got away from them. It was the first time we had really been on our own, and we had much to say. On our return we parted in the shelter of the back-door where no one could see our first hurried kiss. I remember to this day the hammering of my heart as he ran off down the road, and turned to wave goodbye. After this flying visit a lovely diamond half-hoop ring arrived. And as far as Uncle George and Aunt Ellen were concerned that ended the argument.

'In November, dear Aunt Lena (Aunt Ellen's sister, but oh, how different!) invited me to stay at her Bournemouth flat. She had also invited Arthur from Edinburgh that we might get to know each other better. There we discussed dates. It was at first my intention to wait till the following June for the wedding; but I began to have second thoughts. English people did not usually marry in Lent, and Arthur said that Scottish people rather avoided May, so the only convenient time seemed to be in February.

'So 8 February was fixed for the ceremony in St Mary Abbot's, Kensington, which was more convenient than Eastbourne. Mr Gordon having his hands full with church affairs in Edinburgh, it was left to me to make all the arrangements. Many of his Scottish friends came south for the occasion, Richard Brown (poor Richard!), Dr Norman Macleod of Inverness, Sir Colin and Lady Macrae, and many of the Gordon contingent, whom I then met for the first time.

'I had six bridesmaids, in pretty dresses of fawn cashmere silk trimmed with pale rose-pink, and hats of the same colour. They carried lovely bouquets of pink tulips and lilies of the valley and pink heath. Their presents were gold bangles with a monogram of A and O in small pearls and turquoise, which I had designed.

'My dress was of cream ribbed silk, trimmed with pearl passementerie, with a long tulle veil and semi-wreath of real orange-blossom, and a beautiful bouquet. This the Gordon brothers took back to their widowed mother, Lady Gordon, who was unable to make the journey from Edinburgh, but to whom they gave a favourable report of her new daughter-in-law.

'I remember "going away" in a violet dress and picture hat, and short velvet elbow-length cape with feather rucheing, quite the mode at that time. We first only went to Aunt Lena's West End flat before catching the evening train for the Continent. Next day we reached Paris, and on to Mentone for a fortnight. It was a joy to wander through groves of orange and lemon trees full of fruit and blossom. Later we moved on to Florence and Venice, seeing wonderful pictures and churches, and much of interest and beauty in both places. Arthur was everything I had longed for. He still wore his deer-stalking hat, though by now it was clear that the stalking season was at an end!

'A month later we found our way home to Edinburgh.'

4
Edinburgh

Edinburgh's West End is cut through by a steep rocky valley in which the Water of Leith flows towards the seaport of that name some three miles away. At high level the Queensferry Road crosses the valley by the Dean Bridge, under whose shadow the old village of Dean nestles by the waterside. And just down-stream from the bridge, like a small castle perched on a cliff edge, stands the house in Lennox Street where Arthur Gordon had his home. There on 8 March 1893 he picked up his young bride and carried her across the threshold.

In her honour he had had the window-boxes enclosed with glass panels (the latest idea) and filled with potted spring flowers and graceful ferns. Olga thought these somewhat obstructed the lovely view of the flower-beds and shrubberies across the valley, but she refrained from saying so. There was a delightful display of wedding presents in the drawing-room, chiefly in the form of jewellery from the Gordon family. This pleased her greatly as she had very little of her own, most of her mother's having been absorbed among her attentive relations during her childhood. But, greatest surprise of all, there in the drawing-room stood a Steinway Boudoir Grand, the gift of the congregation of St Andrew's. Olga was deeply touched by the kindness of her welcome.

Of course, some of the furnishings were rather austere; the horse-hair sofa and chairs without cushions, the heavy oak book-cases stained almost black; and two enormous gloomy Landseer etchings, 'The Stag at Bay', and 'The Challenge'. The latter depicted a huge stag bellowing across a misty loch at its rival; it seemed to Olga to give undue emphasis to the predominantly male atmosphere of the house. Never mind, she thought, some pretty curtains and cretonnes, and perhaps some delicate flower paintings, will soon restore the balance.

But there was one picture that riveted her attention, 'The Doctor', by Luke Fildes, R.A. In a darkened cottage room a little girl lies feverish on the bed, while her young parents from the far corner gaze with helpless anxiety at the central figure. It is that of the Doctor, seated on a bedside chair, his whole attention concentrated on the little patient, watching for some sign of reaction to his last dose of medicine. Is it too much to suppose that he is praying for divine intervention to save the little life, and incidentally his own reputation? A dramatic situation indeed. Olga could not help feeling a deep ancestral urge, even if veterinary in origin, to play the doctor's part when some day she would have children of her own.

On the first Sunday after their return the congregation were all agog to see the new bride in church. Rumour had been busy because of the foreign flavour of her names, Olga and Constant. Was she French, Russian, Swedish, or even Greek? All were possible to the good folk of St Andrew's whose international awareness did not extend far south of Hadrian's Wall. But when on that first Sunday the Minister's pew was seen to be empty there was wagging of heads. Some whispered charitably that she might have gone to the English Church, though that would pose an awkward social problem. But one, more observant, detected in a back pew a chic little bonnet not quite in the Edinburgh style. It was in fact 'a dainty little brown straw trimmed with coral-pink velvet, and worn with a nut-brown costume with a coral-pink front'. And when, as they gathered outside after the service, the owner of the new bonnet was found to be the Minister's wife, she was soon reassured that she was truly among friends.

Proof of that had been given already, and in the Manse itself of all places. The day before the return of the newly-weds Arthur's hitherto excellent cook-housekeeper and two domestics had left without notice. A kind friend in the congregation saved the situation by quickly engaging a new cook, Mrs Inkster, a good table-maid and a house-maid. Olga brought all her tact to bear and for a short while all went smoothly. Then it became apparent that the formidable Mrs Inkster was bent on assuming control of the household, including also the Minister's young wife. Olga felt the situation required firmness rather than tact, and the inevitable crisis broke when she remarked that she preferred that a baked rice-pudding should be creamy rather than a mixture of dried rice and scrambled eggs. Mrs Inkster was outraged. She announced that if there were to be complaints over such trifles she would have to go. Olga agreed and installed a third cook, this time of her own choosing.

It was the time of the Annual General Assembly of the Church of Scotland, and the Minister of St Andrew's was one of those traditionally expected to offer hospitality to important visitors. Olga had never before acted as hostess, or even been present at a dinner-party; nor was she experienced in the particular niceties of social etiquette current in the Scottish capital. But she was determined that the evening's arrangements should reflect full credit

on Arthur as one of the rising figures in the Church. She
and Arthur drew up a list of twenty guests, among them
their acquaintance Sir Archibald Campbell of Stracathro,
brother of Sir Henry Campbell-Bannerman, the Prime
Minister. Olga, in conference with her newly appointed
cook, decided on the following modest six-course menu:

Mulligatawny Soup

Sole Bonne Femme

Roast Chicken with Chipped Potatoes and Peas

Choufleur au gratin

Ice-Cream

Dessert

When the great day came the guests arrived, were paired
off in order of precedence, and in an orderly procession
entered the dining-room where all took their appointed
seats. So far, so good.

The trouble began with the soup, an unhappy choice.
Olga was engrossed in the conversation of her guest of
honour while soup was being served. When she tasted it
she realised to her horror that the cook had mixed in the
entire pot of mulligatawny paste. Her frantic eye-signals
to the host at the other end of the long table went un-
heeded. At last Arthur took a mouthful, and finding it
like liquid fire urged his guests to leave it alone. Too late.
All were gasping for breath, or stuffing their napkins into
their mouths. The fish course might have been all right,
if anyone had been able to taste it — or anything after it.
But worse was to follow. The entrée of choufleur au gratin
was being handed round with the preceding course of
chicken! The ice-cream, an artistic confection from
MacVitie's in the form of a large green melon, helped to
cool their burning mouths, but the elaborate dessert was
wasted on palates that were numbed.

When the ladies retired to the drawing-room leaving the gentlemen to their wines, Olga apologised most humbly for the disasters of the meal. But everyone was very sympathetic, and told such amusing anecdotes of their own domestic disasters that she was left feeling it did not matter very much after all.

Olga found that in her west-end parish much of her time was taken up with calling on parishioners and thankfully leaving cards if they were out. On her 'at home' days the process was reversed, and she sat in her drawing-room receiving a stream of callers whose visits were fortunately limited by custom to twenty minutes each. There were moments when she wondered if her time could not be better spent, for instance in visiting the poor if there were any; but that of course was the responsibility of the Minister's Assistant who could understand their language.

In August it was a relief to join the usual exodus from town, and leave their home with its windows plastered over with brown paper to mask the cleaning operations that would keep the domestics busy during their absence. Arthur and Olga had taken a house at Connel Ferry, where he taught her the art of sea-fishing with a line from a boat. Olga however insisted that the art of threading a lug-worm on a hook should be reserved for him alone. They also made the trip to Staffa and Iona. Olga never forgot the beauty of Fingal's Cave as she looked down through the clear water at the multi-coloured sea-anemones and waving weed so movingly described in Mendelssohn's Overture.

When they returned to Edinburgh Olga could no longer conceal the fact that 'a little visitor' was to be expected at Christmas. She and her intimate friends in the south set to work on the layette, all to be made by hand. She also started trimming a tall swing-cradle with elaborate muslin frills and curtains. She bought a nursing chair and a large folding screen which she began to cover with bright pictures and coloured postcards.

As the time drew near, and Olga began to find the long walk to St Andrew's Church too much, interest among the ladies of the congregation steadily increased. Dear Aunt Lena was summoned from Eastbourne, for although childless herself she had the priceless gift of imparting confidence and serenity to expectant mothers. And on 23 December Olga's first-born son arrived without undue difficulty. It required no small effort for the proud father to remain straight-faced as he declaimed from the pulpit to a doubly expectant congregation, 'Unto us a child is born, unto us a son is given', a prophecy which was duly confirmed in the Birth columns of *The Times* and the *Scotsman*. Immediately there arrived cards of congratulation with a flood of samples of baby-powders, soaps, and nursery accessories. To the many kind inquirers were sent special silver-printed cards of thanks, each with a miniature card attached, on which was printed the baby's name, Edward Francis Strathearn Gordon, and the date of his arrival.

The following year promised to be a happy one for the family. Arthur's progress from bachelordom to marriage and parenthood raised him in the esteem of his congregation. Olga too was glad to relinquish much of her social life at the call of motherhood and the home. Little Teddy beaming out from the curtains of his cot, found the V.I.P. treatment of a first-born much to his liking and was quick to call attention to any temporary lapse in the service in a voice that could be heard throughout the house. Lady Gordon too, now chair-bound and uncertain of temperament, purred over her grandson, calling him 'my little gold-crested wren'.

But one change was still needed to make their happiness complete. After eight years in a leading city parish, Arthur was finding that administrative pressures and endless committee work took up too much of the time he needed for helping individuals in their troubles. Olga too felt that the country would be a quieter and healthier place for a young family, especially now that another little stranger was due in the following spring. So they prayed for the opportunity of a country parish not too remote from Edinburgh. With commendable promptitude their prayers were answered. The peaceful parish of Monzievaird* in lovely Strathearn was due to become vacant in a few months' time. Seizing the chance, Arthur let it be known that if he were invited there to preach and won the congregation's approval he might be willing to accept a call. And the Elders of Monzievaird, delighted at finding the Minister of so important a city parish rising to their fly, waived the election procedure and forthwith offered him the vacancy with a unanimous vote.

The Gordons visited Monzievaird and were well received by the Elders. But the manse itself posed a challenge. Externally it was a neat early-Victorian building of warm sandstone; but internally the peeling wallpaper and crumbling fireplaces suggested that the Heritors for some years past had regarded maintenance work as an unseemly luxury, having in mind the possible approach of the Day of Judgment. As to the drainage system, to say that it was non-existent would merely be concealing the horrid truth. The house stood upon a system of uncemented stone channels with no outlet in any direction. With questing noses Olga and Arthur explored the ground floor, and everywhere met the same distressing aroma. In those days any disease whose cause was not immediately obvious was attributed to the drains, and when on inquiry they learned that a family who had recently rented the place had all contracted scarlet fever, they exchanged blank looks more expressive than words.

But there was no denying that in other respects it was just what they were looking for. True the money side of it would be difficult. Arthur would have to sacrifice three-quarters of his St Andrew's stipend. To put the house right

*Monzie, like bonnie.

61

with a new drainage system would cost a pretty penny; and the small congregation could not offer much towards it. Never mind, said Olga, she could help with that side of it. So in blind faith they took their decision and accepted the call to take over the parish in the following spring. The Elders were delighted; and after cordial farewells, the Gordons returned to Edinburgh, excited at the future that was opening up before them. But it was not to be so easy as all that.

The winter of 1894–5 was one of the coldest on record. In Lennox Street the water-pipes froze solid. Baths were impossible as all the water had to be carried in buckets over the icy cobbles from a stand-pipe at the end of the street. The kitchen range too was out of action, so there was little warmth in the house and meals had to be boiled over the dining-room fire. Arthur, returning from a Communion service in the Highlands, declared that it was the first time he had seen frost patterns on the Communion Cup.

Before long the extreme cold brought on an epidemic of influenza, and soon nurses were unobtainable. There were many deaths, for the influenza developed all too easily into pneumonia, for which no remedy was known.

Early in March Olga contracted a severe chill and cough, and the doctor after an impressively thorough examination pronounced his verdict — influenza. However, as the baby was not expected for another ten days he expressed the hope that she would be well by then. Three days later Olga's second son was born, with no difficulty except that 'he was found to have an umbilical hernia'. No one seems to have asked why.

A famous surgeon, one of whose qualifications was that he was a friend of the Gordon family, was called in. He advised an immediate operation under chloroform. At a brief service held in the dining-room the baby was baptised with the name of 'Arthur', while preparations for the operation were being made in the adjoining room. Olga 'was shown the wee boy, a sweet fair-haired babe swathed in a shawl', before he went in for his operation. She never saw him again.

On the following day the famous surgeon was still quite optimistic. But when Olga asked her *accoucheur* for his frank opinion she was told the baby was unlikely to survive the week. He proved right. Olga tried to keep a firm grip of herself. Afterwards she remembered Arthur bringing Teddy in to see her; a fair curly-headed toddler of fifteen months, dressed in the little crimson jersey she had knitted for him, with a short white skirt pleated like a kilt. 'Such a picture with his bright eyes and flushed cheeks!' Next day he too was in the grip of influenza. Arthur helplessly watched the fever running high and wondered if they were to lose Teddy as well as the baby. Olga's condition too worsened and she began to be delirious. The monthly nurse said plainly that the work was too much for her. Arthur in desperation sent a telegram to Aunt Lena.

The twelfth of March, the day when the little one's life had been due to begin, was the day when it ended. His father, supported by two brothers (Captain Fred of the Gordon Highlanders, and Huntly, then a law student) went by carriage through the snow-bound streets to the family burial-ground in the Dean Cemetery. He carried in his hands the little coffin of his son, and laid on it a sprig of Gordon ivy and Olga's wreath of snow-drops.

Arthur was near the breaking-point then. Yet somehow in the background other affairs had to be carried on; the winding-up of his work at St Andrew's, with the ceremonies necessary for introducing his successor; the work on Monzievaird Manse, and those awful drains; the arrangements for the move in early May. Afterwards he realised thankfully that all this had helped him to keep sane.

But Olga had none of these distractions. Even Arthur's reading of poetry and the Bible brought her no comfort. She had fought hard to control her emotions, but now the floodgates of her grief broke and were swept aside. The doctors, now more than one, tried every sleeping drug without avail, and then abandoned hope of her recovery. Arthur was advised to dab the back of her neck with acetic acid, which raised a blister; and to apply ice-packs to her head. In her delirium she saw once again the picture in the Wiertz Museum at Brussels of an agonised man thrusting open his own coffin-lid, and like him she cried out, 'I am not dead yet', repeating it many times. One night she kept saying, 'Feed me, feed me', and consumed no less than six tins of Brand's Essence of Chicken. After that she refused all food, and became unconscious.

Then suddenly one evening a cab drew up and disgorged the massive form of Aunt Lena, followed by three nurses. Her placid smile, her genial assumption that everything would soon be all right, affected the distraught household like a blessing. In her black rustling dress she passed majestically round the house, with a tut-tut and a chuckle that drew wan smiles from the domestic staff, the monthly nurse and even from poor Arthur. At her touch Olga awoke and once more became coherent. The three nurses worked in round-the-clock shifts. The monthly nurse took charge of Teddy, whose fever abated.

April brought milder weather and a gradual return to normal life. The epidemic ended and Aunt Lena, her life-saving mission complete, returned to the South Coast. Olga, having regained her balance, consoled herself by lavishing a double share of mother love on little Teddy, which was perhaps not entirely for his good. And when Arthur one day found her surrounded by books of sample wallpapers, with a respectful representative of the decorators in attendance, he saw that the battle was over, and sighing with relief praised God from the depths of his heart.

5
Monzievaird

Monzievaird, the Cornfield of the Bards, is indeed a lovely spot, 'the sweetest neuk in all Strathearn', as a previous Minister called it. In those days it was barely a hamlet, just the church, the Manse, the schoolhouse and a couple of cottages; and now that the church has been demolished the heart of it is gone. But still the houses stand with the Grampian Mountains behind them, and look southwards across the cornfields and the river to Torlum, a hill that obligingly wears a warning cap of cloud whenever rain is to be expected.

The Manse stands back some distance from the road, with a large sunken garden in front of it, full of old fruit trees and box hedges. In those days it was a peaceful and secluded place. One might perhaps have heard the churring of a horse-drawn hay-cutter out in the fields, and MacGregor busy with his lawn-mower round the house to have it tidy for the new Minister and his lady; and old Maclean, the stone-breaker, tap-tapping away with his long hammer at the heap of road-metal down at the drive entrance. Occasionally there would be the slow trudging hoofs of a shire-horse and the grinding wheels of the laden farm-cart; and very occasionally the sprightly clippity-clop of a carriage rolling smartly along the road to the Comrie shops raising a small dust-cloud behind it. There would be a background of bird song and the murmur of bees among the lilac bushes; and that was about all.

To Monzievaird Manse, looking its best in the sunshine of early June, came Olga and Arthur, with little Teddy and his Nannie. It would perhaps be easy here for them to forget the smoke and fog of 'Auld Reekie' throughout that bitter winter; less easy, but at least possible, to start forgetting their private tragedy, for the world must go on. So hand-in-hand they went from room to room, Olga delighting to see the new decorations, planned by her in Edinburgh and supervised by Arthur on his occasional visits to their new home. The builders from Comrie had worked with a will and finished the job on time, and Olga laughed as he told her how the Evil Spirit of the Drains had been exorcised with bell, book and candle; and agreed that the whole house now smelt fresh for the first time, and indeed sweet from the welcoming bunches of lilac that Mrs MacGregor had arranged in it.

The little church was filled on Sunday with an expectant congregation of farmers and labourers and their families. All were dressed in their Sunday best, many of the men wearing white celluloid collars, their hair shiny with pomade. There was a good sprinkling too of the lairds and their friends from some of the big estates in the parish; and many stopped afterwards to give their personal welcome to their elected Minister and his wife. It was a happy gathering and just the encouragement that Olga needed as she began the country life that had long been her dream.

To begin with she wanted to be able to get about quickly

and easily, so she decided she must have a bicycle. But first 'one was very careful to have a tailor-made costume specially made for cycling in decency'. Only when that was settled to her satisfaction did she buy a lady's bicycle with an intricate string guard around the back wheel, and start learning to ride. At first, as she steered an unsteady course along the road, there were some surprised comments at what seemed contrary to nature, but before long it was accepted as an amusing form of harmless exercise and certainly the quickest way to Comrie and back.

Next she bought a riding pony and side-saddle costume to go with it, and after that a pony ('Judy') to go in the trap which Arthur taught her to drive. Then she bought a covered waggonette for station use; and finally for best occasions a Victoria, an open carriage with folding hood and a box on which the coachman sat with a waterproof rug over his knees and a long carriage whip at his side. 'Punch' was the big carriage horse that drew the last two vehicles. The coachman, resplendent in dark green coat with brass buttons and a top hat, was none other than MacGregor, the Minister's Man, gardener and cowman, who regarded his elevated position as well suited to a veteran of the Ashanti wars.

While Arthur went about his work in the parish in a more individual way than had been possible in Edinburgh's West End, Olga concentrated on country skills. The friendly cow, grazing in the glebe, gave an abundance of milk and cream from which Mrs MacGregor, the coachman's wife, taught her to make butter and cheese. She kept hens too so that there was always a good supply of eggs and chickens. Helped by the beadle's son, she set about the deserted garden, and within a couple of years had it back in full production. The soil was rich, the garden sheltered. Gradually the fruit trees recovered and she was even rewarded with wall-grown peaches ripened in the open. And many were the gifts of strawberries, blackcurrants and raspberries from the Manse garden that reached those who were less well off.

In 1897 two events occurred whose historical significance was not fully apparent at the time. It was the year of
the dear old Queen's Diamond Jubilee, and for some
reason she decided that the title 'Honourable' should be
conferred on the sons and daughters of Legal Life Peers,
ranking them after Barons and before Baronets. Thus our
unassuming little family became not just 'gentry' and
'carriage-folk', but 'titled'; not that it made the slightest
difference to them. But for MacGregor, the coachman, it
certainly did; for he was now entitled by custom to wear a
cockade in his top hat, and that was a distinction that put
him above most other coachmen in the parish.

The other event concerned Olga and 'Judy', as they set
off for Comrie with the pony-cart. Suddenly rounding a
corner, Judy saw a carriage approaching her without any
visible horses, though their snorting and puffing was
frighteningly loud. Terrified by this apparition Judy
swerved off the road, crossed the ditch and tried to get
through the hedge. When the ghost-carriage had gone Olga
got her back on the road, where she stood wild-eyed and
trembling, and finally had to be led back to the stables. It
was for both of them the first time the horse was displaced
by the internal combustion engine. As MacGregor con-
temptuously remarked, 'Ach, who would want a contraption the like o' yon!'

Another event was recorded in Olga's notes as follows:

The first event of family importance in 1898 was the birth on
February 23rd of a third son; but not without some anxiety to
my family, who wondered what might happen after my previous
very serious illness. However all went well, in spite of a scare of
scarletina at the Manse stables.

This time there was no advance publicity about a little
stranger being expected; no reference to doctors or nurses,
no visit from Aunt Lena, or silver-printed cards of thanks;
not even a mention of the baby's name. Just 'all went well',
particularly down at the stables.

It is hardly likely that this little stranger arrived trailing clouds of glory; more probably he travelled by second-class stork. But either way he had a soft and happy landing among the cornfields. And now, having broken gently to the reader the identity of the third son, I can at last join the party myself and give to Arthur and Olga the names I really knew them by — Father and Mother.

I was indeed lucky in my parents. Mother had a constant urge to enjoy life and help others to do so, even though some of them perhaps felt they were being a little over-organised. Father too liked to keep up the tradition of his great-grandfather Adam of Griamachary who, you remember, was 'given to hospitality, and to all comers and goers from the highest to the lowest could furnish a plentiful and hospitable table and lodgings'.

Christmas Days at the Manse meant friends sharing the full English dinner with turkey and champagne. But New Year's Day was the great day for the Scots. Mother started a Highland Games in the field opposite the Manse to which all villagers in the parish were welcomed. The sporting side was organised by the school Dominie and some of the leading villagers. Mother laid on the refreshments, supplying 'huge jugs of boiling cocoa and quantities of sandwiches and buns to keep the crowd fed and happy. We were usually blessed with a bright frosty day, which was spent in innocent enjoyment and was a counter attraction to idle hours in the Comrie pubs.' I am not sure that Old Adam would have entirely approved of boiling cocoa or this high Victorian ideal of moral betterment. But times change, and it was natural that at the Manse a firm stand should be taken against the Demon Drink.

We also held occasional soirées at the Manse with dancing and reels in the dining-room to the strains of a fiddle played by MacGregor's brother who lived across the valley. Amusing readings by the Minister were also a welcome addition, and music at the piano by his wife. A wonderful supper was arranged with hot coffee and cold dainties, jellies and creams in the kitchen, which was fully disguised and transformed into a Supper Room. It was an exhausting time for the Organiser [she wrote], but was always remembered as a very happy time by old and young.

But life in the parish was not always sweetness and light. There was the case of the eccentric Colonel Bagshot of Drummore, wealthy and handsome with carefully cultivated Dundreary whiskers, but a poseur, secretly cruel to his wife and dependants, a man dominated by a desire for notoriety and power, a wicked neighbour with an explosive temper, and in Father's calculated words 'a renowned and treacherous bully'. He had bought the Drummore estate, married and retired there, and on the strength of having once been a Lieutenant in the Volunteers, assumed the title of full Colonel of a Guards Regiment.

An earlier Minister of Monzievaird had evidently displeased him in some way, and the Colonel decided to teach him a lesson. He came to the Manse when the Minister was out, and announced he would await him in his study; from which he then removed all possible means of self-defence. On the Minister's return the Colonel produced a large hunting-crop, and 'administered no mere nominal horse-whipping' but an attack so violent and brutal that he left the poor man unconscious on the floor. In due course he was apprehended, tried, and sent to gaol for several months. On release he returned to his position in the county unabashed, and with what Father called 'his usual unparalleled effrontery' tried to pose as an injured innocent.

The effrontery grew no less with the passing years. When King Edward VII was about to inspect the Veterans of the Crimea and the Indian Mutiny assembled on the esplanade of Edinburgh Castle, Colonel Bagshot arrived uninvited in full uniform and took station so that he might be the first to receive the royal greeting. King Edward noticed his absence of medals, took in the situation at a glance and began his hand-shaking with a real veteran of the name of Sandy MacBeth, a deer-stalker from Atholl. No rebuke could have been more courteous or effective. Father regarded the Colonel as Vesuvius, a formidable landmark, but one best kept at a distance. They met at times, but for some reason never clashed openly.

I can now confess that as I grew up this shocking story of the Colonel horse-whipping the Minister in the Manse study used to cause me some secret amusement. The study was quite a small room, and to wield a carriage whip in it would have been a difficult matter. I used to picture the portly and breathless Colonel pursuing the Minister round and round ('Gad, Sir, wait till I catch you!') and having to stop and disentangle his whip from the gas-brackets every time he flourished it. It was only on reading Father's papers that I realised the Colonel's weapon was a heavy hunting crop, and rather less than funny.

During the South African War soldiers were always welcome at the Manse. When a crippled Scottish soldier by the name of Colin Campbell came to the door for help he was of course received with Christian kindness. The poor chap said he had been wounded in both legs at the battle of Colenso. Colin was made as comfortable as possible in our spare bedroom. He was given a new outfit of clothes, and a new pair of crutches was ordered. He was taken out for drives in our carriage, which seemed to cheer his flagging spirits greatly. Meanwhile Father set about finding a vacancy in a convalescent home.

By degrees Colin let it be known that his past life had not been a blameless one; but he was very repentant, and surely his bravery at Colenso atoned for all that. He had an unusual knowledge of Bible texts, so it was not surprising that under Mother's prayerful influence he soon became a reformed character. He loved to sing hymns, and it was a touching sight to see him with tear-stained cheeks singing that old favourite 'Yield not to temptation for yielding is sin', while Mother, equally moved, pedalled

71

hard to keep up with him on the harmonium in the dining-room.

Our wounded hero stayed with us for three weeks, until Father secured his admission to the Princess Louise Nursing Home. Then from that comfortable haven Colin wrote a letter to Princess Louise herself making such scandalous charges of his ill-treatment by the doctors and nurses that the Princess asked the police to make enquiries. Alas, they unearthed such a story that Colin was soon back on the streets again. We also discovered that some of our best silver spoons and forks were missing: but Father declined to prosecute.

The inquiry revealed that Colin had never fought in the South African War at Colenso or anywhere else. He was in fact a Danish seaman whose legs had been broken in an accident in the South Seas. He owned to nineteen previous convictions for fraud. It had been the Bible Society at Singapore that with the best of intentions had launched him on a career of crime. When he had left hospital they employed him to sell Bibles at fifty cents each, and paid him two dollars commission on every copy sold. At first the Bible Society was much gratified at the remarkable improvement in Bible sales that followed this arrangement. But they were less pleased on finding that Colin had achieved these record results, and greatly increased his own earnings, by quietly sinking packages of Bibles in Singapore harbour.

Colin Campbell finished his time in Edinburgh as a professional beggar on crutches (*our* crutches!) with a regular pitch at the top of the Waverley Steps. Though born too soon for the Welfare State, he continued to extract a satisfactory living from society in his own way. In his dealings with us it was he who had the last word, when he wrote a letter to Father in the following terms:

Rev. Sir,

    I come to Edin. on purpose in spite of you. Scotland have not

kill me yet. You have tried to keep me down to the very point
of the Laws. I ask if that is Christianity. You send notice to the
police in Scotland. I did not rob your property on purpose, but I
am sorry I told you false. Now I am settle in Edin. comfortable in
a good situation through a kind Christian lady. Don't you call
yourself Christian any more.

Goodbye and God dam you.

Alfred Collinson or Campbell

Father, being only human, boiled when he read this. He
was particularly hurt at the false accusation that he had
put the police on to him. Then, remembering his position,
he just sighed and turned the other cheek.

Meanwhile Mother, who believed in looking ahead, already
had other irons in the fire.

Our family income in those days was about £1,500 a
year. This was more than enough to meet the needs of our
family of four, as well as normal wages and keep for a
nurse, a cook, a parlour-maid, a house-maid and MacGregor
the coachman-gardener whose wife also ran the laundry.
They all made up a happy household, and only at rare
intervals did one of them leave us to get married.

On the advice of Richard Brown, Father's chartered
accountant friend, Mother decided to invest her surplus
funds in house property. She was thinking that in a few
years' time the family might move back nearer to Edinburgh when her two young sons would be needing a good
education. After some exploring her choice fell on the
little seaside town of North Berwick, near enough to
Edinburgh, and she engaged a leading Edinburgh architect
to build her a house there overlooking the Ladies' Golf
Links. It was a fine house called Strathearn Lodge, well
furnished, and it attracted as its first tenant Prince Edward
of Saxe-Weimar and family. They paid the incredible sum
of £100 a month for July and August, and were joined
there at times by the Prince of Wales (later King Edward

VII). So in her activity of property-owning landlady, Mother started near the top. Of course we children knew nothing of this at the time. Even when the house became our family home, she never told us. She was no snob — at least not consciously. And we were thus not overawed by the thoughts of any royal predecessors in our home. ('Who's been sleeping in *my* bed?' the Little Bear might have wondered, testing the springs.)

But to return to the Manse, and my eldest brother Teddy. Mother recorded that in very early years he learnt his alphabet from illustrated wooden blocks, and was quick at word-building and reading. It was our family tradition that Gordon sons should be able to read the 23rd Psalm to their parents on their fifth birthday. Mother would not allow that to be just a matter of memory. She dodged about on the difficult words, which Teddy considered hardly fair; though, knowing what he was up against, he had made specially sure of them beforehand. Soon after he was five, he could read simple sentences and, in Mother's words, his intelligence often outran the mentality of a simple country nurse. But actually he made his first public impact long before his fifth birthday.

It is customary for Protestant (or perhaps I should say Presbyterian) Ministers when in the pulpit to wear double linen bands hanging down from the collar. These are known as Geneva Bands, and represent the Cloven Tongues of Fire with which it is hoped the Minister is endowed by the Holy Spirit at his ordination. Little Teddy's contribution to this mystery, at his first attendance in Monzievaird Church, was to ask in a piercing voice, 'Why has Father got his bib on?' He was forcibly removed, protesting all the way down the aisle.

What is the first thing you can remember? My earliest recollection is that of being balanced on the icy rim of 'the article' and repeatedly asked, 'Have you done your duty yet?' which inquiry would be met with a non-committal silence. Periodically Mother lifted me off and either effusively congratulated or replaced me in disgrace. What a way to start the day! My interest in the article was more as a means of self-propulsion backwards across the nursery floor, a purpose for which frequent over-balancings showed it to have been ill-suited.

When it came to dressing her small sons, Mother was evidently swayed by conflicting considerations; her own idea of what looked romantic or attractive; the Victorian fashion in Highland (fancy) dress; what was practical and economical; what materials she had to spare, for she made many of her own clothes herself; and her ingenuity in adapting Teddy's cast-offs for my use. The results were sometimes surprising.

There is a photograph of Teddy, at eighteen months, in a wide-spread coat and rakish furry hat, looking like an infant version of Henry VIII. A tinted miniature of me at the same age shows a mass of golden curls overflowing an elaborate collar of antique lace on a frock of green velvet. The face wears an uneasy smile.

Teddy at seven and I at two and a half appear together in a surviving snapshot. Teddy has a Glengarry bonnet, an ill-fitting kilt, tartan stockings, and a plain coat that seems to have shrunk in the wash. His triumphant smile suggests that he has won the argument for improved dress, and is wearing the coat for the last time. The small figure at his side wears a Balmoral bonnet with a red 'toorie' on top, a sailor's double-breasted jacket, and a shapeless skirt extending far below my stocking-covered knees. It suggests perhaps that Mother had intended me to be a daughter.

But two years later a studio portrait was done of me in full Highland rig, seated on a cardboard rock against a painted background of roses and aspidistras. I wore a black velvet jacket with silver buttons, a Gordon kilt with a horse-hair sporran, and a Glengarry bonnet with our silver badge of the Boar's Head, bearing the motto 'Forward without Fear'.

It is perhaps a relief to turn from this Dee-side finery, which none the less I was proud to wear, to a portrait of Helena aged two and a half. It is a charming half-length nude, showing a serious little angel, wearing only a red coral necklace. Even Solomon in all his glory. . . .

The South African War was a constant topic in those days. My part in it was to go stamping round the nursery, firing a pop-gun and shouting 'Bang, Kruger!' Kruger was of course that shifty patriarch in black frock coat and top hat who was President of the Boer Republic. Shortly after this Kruger fled, leaving the war to be carried on for a further two years by other Boer leaders who appear to have escaped my notice.

About that time I found myself fighting at the battle of Spion Kop. My brother, four years older, of course impersonated the dauntless British defending the mound of that name in the Manse garden. To me was allotted the unpopular role of the attacking Boers. I duly advanced up the slope, and on hearing him shout, 'Bang! You're dead', fell in a death agony on the lawn. Unfortunately I fell across the hole of an underground wasps' nest, from which the enraged occupants emerged in a swarm and quickly made my agony a very lively one. Mother carried me yelling to the laundry and daubed my exposed parts with the blue-bag; and thus I lived to fight another day.

Mother was naturally eager to bring out her musical talent in her children. Teddy was acute enough to dodge that one. It was I who fell for it, having been observed beating time to somebody's singing. So I must be taught a song, and of course it had to be a Scottish song, chosen by my patriotic romantic Father. My parlour trick took this form. Father would sit on the drawing-room sofa with one leg across the other; I sat on his foot facing him and holding his outstretched hands. The foot then provided the bouncing motion of a cantering horse, while we sang together:

To the Lords of Convention 'twas Claverhouse spoke,
Ere the King's Crown go down there are crowns to be broke;
And let each cavalier who loves honour and me,
Come follow the bonnet of Bonnie Dundee!

> Come fill up my cup, come fill up my can,
> Come saddle your horses and call out your men.
> Come open the West Port and let me gang free,
> And it's 'Hey for the bonnets of Bonnie Dundee!'

Whereupon Bonnie Dundee with a war-whoop would roll off his horse and land on the carpet. I hadn't the slightest idea what it all meant; but I loved it, and there were cries of, 'More, more!'

When on several occasions this trick had earned me some applause from guests and parents Teddy must have felt that his position as the bright one, the apple of Mother's eye, was slipping a little and he meditated revenge. One day under promise of secrecy he took me to the dining-room side-board, opened a cupboard and drew out a triple silver cruet. The salt I knew, also the pepper; but what was in the tall bottle? As a special treat Teddy drew out the tiny silver spoon full of lovely red pepper. 'Is it nice?' I asked. 'Try it,' he replied, nodding encouragement. I took it fearlessly. Apparently on fire, I ran screaming to Mother, who gave me a cup of water and told me to wash out my mouth. Her rebuke of Teddy, 'that wasn't very kind', struck me as less than adequate, which is probably why I still remember the incident.

There was another occasion when my own literal-mindedness, combined with the peculiar humour of grown-ups, resulted in a misunderstanding. Doctor Playfair of St Andrew's was at that time one of the great pillars of the Church of Scotland, and he honoured us by coming to tea. It was a summer afternoon and we had it on the lawn. The Doctor arrived, a positive giant of a man, clad all in black. I took station slightly behind Mother while the introductions were made. Then perceiving me, the Doctor felt it was a moment for jocularity.

'And who is this?' he demanded in a deep rumbling voice.

'This is my second son, Huntly,' replied Father, chucking me under the chin in a way that jerked my head up (a maddening habit!).

The Black Giant rose up on his toes, stretched his great black arms in the air above me, and roared, 'I think I'm going to eat you!' At that moment he looked just like the picture of Apollyon in the *Pilgrim's Progress*, and showed every sign of carrying out his threat. With a terrified yell I got behind mother, and prepared to run for my life; only to be told not to be so silly. But I really think the Doctor looked as silly as I did, trying to explain his merry joke. Distrusting him, I kept well out of his reach as long as he was with us.

But on the whole those were happy days, with drives and picnics in the glens, the climbing of hill-sides and fishing in the burns. On Sundays there was acting, usually of Bible stories. 'Peter in Prison' was one of the best (Acts, 12). Of course Teddy was Peter, and Prison was under the piano. Mother had to impersonate alternately the Angel and Rhoda. I was tried as Rhoda, but as I didn't really understand the part I just had to sit on the floor and be the audience and noises-off. Teddy got the best parts. He was very good as David, but Father's collapse on the sofa as the stricken Goliath brought the loudest encores from the audience. Once when David was wanted he was found to be eating cake in the kitchen. Mother called out, 'If you don't come at once I'll shut you out.' To which, with full mouth he replied, 'Very well then, I shall just be the foolish virgins and stay outside.'

Father was not only good as Goliath, he was pretty good in the pulpit as well, though I didn't understand much of it at the time. His papers show that he was four times summoned to preach to the Queen at Balmoral. The first time was in 1887, her Golden Jubilee Year, only five years after he had been ordained. He tried not to show any nervousness when facing the figure of the little lady dressed in black with a grey feather in her bonnet. Afterwards when she inquired if he had found it something of an ordeal, he replied that he regarded it as a very great privilege. She laughed and recalled another preacher who had shown signs of nervousness: 'I was *so* sorry for him. I nearly threw my Bible over the gallery front to create a diversion in his favour!'

At that time Princess Beatrice, the Queen's youngest daughter, had given birth at Balmoral to her first child, later to be Queen of Spain; and Father was asked to suggest a Highland name for the first princess born in Scotland since the Union with England. Thinking no doubt of Bonnie Prince Charlie's heroine and rescuer, he suggested 'Flora'. It was an unfortunate choice, 'at once pronounced unacceptable from the recollection of poor Lady Flora Hastings, who was so sadly misjudged', and eventually the name Ena was chosen. Next Sunday at the Queen's wish the baby was christened in Crathie Church by the Dean of the Order of the Thistle and Mr Campbell the Parish Minister. This was the Queen's way of showing that she was as truly Queen of Scotland as of England. But there were some murmurs in ecclesiastical circles south of the Border at the thought of the baptismal vessel from which royal babies were customarily christened being entrusted to Scottish Presbyterian hands.

The last time Father preached at Crathie was on 10 June 1900 within eight months of the Queen's death, and these were some of his impressions of that occasion:

Though her eye was dimmed by years and she used a large magnifying glass to follow the hymns, her voice was clear and beautiful. Though lame enough to use a wheel-chair, she insisted in rising to her feet to join in the Lord's Prayer.

When I obeyed the summons to dine at Balmoral that evening,

I found in the drawing-room the Countess of Antrim who told me the Queen had just announced a change of plans. 'We are not going to the Riviera after all,' she had said, 'I am going to Dublin to show my Irish people what I think of the gallantry and devotion of their soldiers.' [In due course the Irish people brushed aside the evil advice of their rebel leaders and gave to the splendid pluck of the octogenarian Queen in her final year the warmest reception she ever won.]

Naturally the Boer War bulked largest in all our minds, and I had referred in my sermon to the recent capture of Pretoria by Lord Roberts. After dinner when I ventured to speak of the great improvement in the war situation since Black Week last December [at which time the Queen had said to Arthur Balfour, 'Please understand that there is no one depressed in *this* house. We are not interested in the possibilities of defeat.'] , she replied, 'I noticed, Mr Gordon, that you did not assume that the taking of Pretoria must needs be the end of the war. I am satisfied that it will go on for many months yet.' The great experience of the Queen had well gauged the tenacity of most of the Boer leaders.

We entered the dining-room to find her already seated, and were shown to our places. After the meal we all returned to the drawing-room, the men and ladies together. To my surprise, Her Majesty walked across to me, smiled and began the conversation by asking after my soldier brother Frederick, who had just been gazetted Brigade Major in the Gordon Highlanders. Very small of stature was the widow of Windsor and Balmoral, but she was easy to talk to if you spoke straight and to the point. When I referred to the albums on her table containing photographs of all the officers killed at the Front, I shall never forget the pathetic emphasis of her beautiful voice as she said, 'It is terrible to think how many brave men have fallen; *dear* General Wauchope, and Colonel Downman of the Gordons, whom I liked so much when they were here last year, and many another fine fellow.' She had the tenderest of hearts, and the privates no less than the officers engaged her sympathies. Understandably so, as she was herself a soldier's daughter.

She knew my parish was in Strathearn, and I told her of one of our local characters, Sir David Baird, who had taken the Cape of Good Hope from the Dutch in 1806 with the loss of only 37 men who were drowned in the landing; and of how when he was taken prisoner at Seringapatam and chained to his Indian prison-guards, his mother on hearing of it, remarked, 'God help the chiel wha's shackled tae oor Davie!' I concluded, 'We of Strathearn are proud to remember that Your Majesty is a *daughter* of Strathearn.' 'Yes, of course I am. My Father was Duke of Kent and Strathearn, and my third son is Duke of Connaught and Strathearn.' We went on jointly to recall her visit to Perthshire in 1842; Taymouth to Killin, under Breadalbane's guidance down Glenogle to Loch Earn, St Fillan's, Dunira, past Monzievaird, Ochtertyre, and on to Drummond Castle. And not one place or person had that wonderful memory forgotten in fifty-eight years!

Many other personalities she spoke of, both in the Army and the Church of Scotland. Her mind and memory were prodigious for any topic, for events, places and people. 'The *ablest* woman I have ever met' was Disraeli's judgment, which I heard in the privacy of my Father's house. 'The most *truthful* woman I have ever known,' said John Bright, the Quaker; and both were right. I still treasure as a keepsake her £5 note, the last contribution that dear hand put in the Church Bag in Scotland.

But if the Queen could inspire Father's devotion, so too could the poorest in the parish find in him their champion.

It was lunch time at the Manse when the front door bell rang. 'Huntly, go and see who that is,' said Mother, who was busy helping out one of her delicious creamy fish pies. On a seat in the front porch I found a fearsome figure, whom at first I took to be a witch. It was an old woman, with a dirty brown wrinkled face; she wore a tattered felt hat on her bedraggled grey hair, and her dirty clothes were covered by an old black shawl which she clutched about her with skinny hands. I could see her toes through her gaping boots. 'Summat tae eat?' she asked.

Running back into the dining-room, I told mother of this apparition. She gave me a full plate of the fish pie, which I took back to the porch and handed to the old woman. 'I'll get you a knife and fork,' I said, but she couldn't wait. Her dirty fingers dug into the rich pie and she began stuffing it into her mouth. She was as ravenous as a starving animal. At that moment Father appeared and I was glad to get back to the dining-room, for her terrible appearance and behaviour frightened me. That is all I can remember; the rest of the story I take from Father's papers.

Her name was Jenny Goudie, and she lived in a tumble-down cottage in the Strowan woods with her idiot son. In our parish the Poor Law Assessment was 2½d. in the pound; and as these were our only two resident paupers, we could well have afforded more than the 4s. 6d. poor relief, which was all the money they had to live on. Jenny was quite harmless. She had her cottage and a few sticks of firewood from the Strowan woods. She asked nothing more than to be let live in her prized seclusion, and neither the laird nor his tenant wished her to be disturbed. Father had visited her from time to time, and with his own hands had done his best to patch up her cottage to keep the rain out, though mother had teased him, saying he couldn't hit a nail on the head. Jenny and her son had been ill with influenza, and the doctor whom Father sent had prescribed a bottle of port wine. Father brought it to them in several medicine bottles which he labelled 'The Red Medicine', for they never touched Intoxicant of any kind. How could they on 4s. 6d. a week for two?

Recently the Poor Law Inspector had visited Jenny. He had been rude to her, and had had the rough side of her tongue in return. In the end he had said he would put them both in the Crieff Poor House. At this Jenny threatened to drown herself in the Earn, and the Dominie told Father she might well do that. But now in her fear of the Inspector she had come to the Manse for help.

That year the Chairman of the Parish Council was 'Colonel' Bagshot. Father took him to see her, and at the time he had no criticism to make. But when the Parish Council met, the Colonel decided that Jenny and her son should be got rid of. He charged this mother of about seventy and her imbecile son with incest, and Father with encouraging it. He stopped their 4s. 6d. a week allowance, and gave notice that they would be evicted from their cottage in three months' time. And owing to inter-estate jealousies, the voting on the Parish Council produced deadlock. Father kept his temper and waited.

After the meeting he enlisted the help of three Elders of the Church and together they arranged for a little wooden hut to be built in the wood close to the old cottage. Jenny transferred to the new abode and Father paid her the 4s. 6d. to the end of the year. Then he got up a Petition to the Local Government Board for Scotland for an inquiry into the case. At first the local Inspector refused to pass it on. But he changed his mind when Father informed him this would lead to his dismissal.

When the Inspector from Edinburgh arrived, the local Inspector had changed his tune. He said he had all along wanted to get Jenny more money, and he had only hesitated to recommend it for fear she would spend it on drink. So at last Jenny's allowance was raised to 6s. a week.

The whirligig of time before long brought its revenge. Within a year the local Inspector, that apostle of temperance, was found on the railway track so drunk that the train had to be stopped while he was moved out of harm's way. Finally when the School Board, of which the people had asked that Father should be appointed Chairman, next met in the Inspector's own house they had before them a letter from Colonel Bagshot reporting that he too had found the Inspector drunk on the roadside. The Inspector admitted 'having had refreshment', and only when hard pressed was driven to accept the words 'to excess'. This was formally recorded in the minutes with a solemn warning for the future, all in the Inspector's own handwriting; whereupon the incident was finally regarded as closed.

I feel it is worth recording here a story about Sir David Baird. During the early part of last century wooded hills in residential parts of Scotland were all too commonly used as bases for monuments to famous men of the time. The monumental inscriptions often included such phrases as 'Erected by his grateful tenants'; though whether the lack of such a public expression of gratitude would have made any difference to the monument's erection is, as they say, a moot point. Near Monzievaird, some three miles west of Crieff, there is such a wooded hill with a high stone obelisk on its summit, commemorating General Sir David Baird. Its name is Tom-a-Chastile, the Peak with the Castle, a name which veils a little-known but dramatic piece of Scottish history.

If you could divest the hill of its trees it would be seen towering steeply up to a craggy top, crowned with the base of a small castle which now supports the granite pinnacle. This beyond doubt was the ancient Castle of Earn, stronghold of the powerful Earls of Strathearn. From this eminence the flames of its beacon-fire would have sent their alerting message across hills and valleys for many miles around. And here it was that in the summer of 1320 (six years after Bannockburn) Agnes, Dowager Countess of Strathearn, looking down from her castle walk on the Earn's well-stocked pools below, darkly conspired with certain other nobles against the life of King Robert the Bruce. Only two months previously Bruce had been confirmed as King by the Scottish Nobles, Clergy and Commons in the famous Declaration of Arbroath; and he may well have been on the lookout for some counterplot. It was certainly no time for any carelessness on the part of the conspirators.

But the plot was discovered. In August 1320 the conspirators, Lord de Soulis, David de Brechin and the Countess Agnes, were tried by the Black Parliament at Scone. The former were both executed for high treason, and the Countess was sentenced to perpetual imprisonment in her own castle. Some time afterwards the castle was set on fire, though whether accidentally or deliberately is not known, and according to legend the Countess perished in the flames.

Five centuries passed. The castle was never rebuilt. And in the early 1800s many of its stones were brought down into the valley for the repair of cottages and dykes.

Then in 1829 General Sir David Baird, the impetuous hero of the Nile, the Cape of Good Hope, Corunna and Seringapatam, died at his home of Ferntower and was buried in Monzievaird churchyard. As late as 1900, old people in the parish still recalled the extraordinary storm of thunder and torrential rain which signalised the occasion. This had naturally been taken as a sign that his fiery spirit was protesting at his burial in such an unsuitably peaceful spot. There was therefore little surprise when his widow decided that his remains should be moved, and that a massive granite obelisk should be erected to his memory on the summit of Tom-a-Chastile. The workmen, anxious that its foundation should be set on solid rock, used gunpowder to clear away the last of the castle stones. And when the dust of the explosion had cleared, great was their astonishment when they found themselves looking down into a dungeon, deep in the solid rock. For there, revealed to view after five centuries, lay all that remained of the proud and daring Agnes, Dowager Countess of Strathearn and Princess of the Orkneys. A sword-hilt was found, with corroded pieces of old armour; some harness-buckles and a pair of stirrups that she did not have the chance to use; and, half-hidden in blackened mould and charred debris, a human skeleton, with a gold bracelet and fragments of ancient ornaments from a lady's dress.

Reluctant to leave the reader on this rather gruesome note, I will add a personal story, which is at least true if not strictly relevant. Some years ago it occurred to me to try out the Earn's 'well-stocked pools', which as far as I know never yielded much reward to Father while we were at Monzievaird.

I fished for a while with a sunken fly and no result. Then, suddenly, came a heart-stopping pull on the line. I tightened steadily, but it was no ordinary fish that surfaced. As it came towards the bank it was clear what had given this bite, for there grinning at me from a bunch of green weed was a gleaming set of false teeth.

After some thought, it occurred to me that there might be rather more to it than that. In fact, one more cast might attach me firmly to the owner of the teeth. Appalled at the thought, I quickly took down my rod, and proceeded to the Comrie Police Station. The Sergeant glanced at me, raised one eyebrow, and said, 'Yes?'

'No,' I replied firmly, 'but I wish to make a statement.' He took up a pen, giving me a distinctly fishy look.

'I have reason to believe', I said, 'that there is a body in the river.' He wrote impassively, while I described the pool and handed him my evidence, the teeth. There was a long pause, with some heavy breathing. He seemed curiously unimpressed.

'Well,' I asked, 'aren't you going to detain me to help the police with their inquiries?'

'No need for that,' he replied gravely. 'We'll let you know if the owner claims them. There may be a small reward.'

'I doubt if he's in a position to offer a reward,' said I, and left the police station, a free man.

To date there has been no reward; nor have I ever fished the Earn again. And why? The Comrie Branch of the Scottish Women's Rural Institute in their booklet describing the village (published 1966) have put it on record that some two thousand years ago the Greek geographer Strabo described the habitable globe as extending from the Ethiopian Circle in the south, to the Earn in the north. Well, they should know. But Strabo presumably had some good reason to remember this small river's name. Something unforgettable must have happened to him when last he fished it. And I would prefer not to be seen standing on the river-bank with his ghost looking over my shoulder. It might frighten the fish.

6
North Berwick

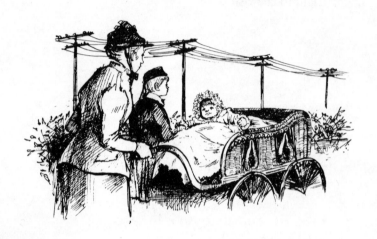

The turn of the century brought many changes to our quiet country lives. In 1897 Mother and Father had already been abroad on a tour of Germany and Austria. Early in 1901 they were off again, this time on a holiday trip to Greece and Egypt.

When their ship reached Piraeus for Athens, their first port of call, they found the Greek people mourning the death of their Queen. They joined them in expressions of sympathy; and it was some time before they learnt with a shock that it was Queen Victoria who had gone. To the Greeks she was not only Britain's great Queen; she was their own pillar of peace in Europe, and they mourned her passing with a sense of political unease. In Athens everyone was already wearing black, and Mother had to hunt from shop to shop before she could find any suitable mourning dress.

In Egypt it was much the same. The Cairo shops were

draped in black. Even at Luxor, far up the Nile, the Fellahin who tilled the soil were saying, 'The Great White Queen is dead. She has done us much good. She has delivered us from oppression and has given us just and merciful rule.' And at the Memorial Service, after the Seaforth Highlanders had fired their last salute across the waters of the Nile, the pipers' lament 'Lochaber no more' moved to tears not only many of the Highlanders, but many of the Egyptian onlookers, too.

Before going abroad Mother had to dispose of her family. She entrusted her 'irrepressible first-born' as a boarder to two elderly Canadian sisters who were starting a girls' school in North Berwick. My nurse and I were consigned to the two old Aunts at Tunbridge Wells, and there spent a couple of months in a state of suspended animation. When the family reassembled at Monzievaird our parents decided that in the following year we should return to the Edinburgh district. This was partly in order to be near suitable boys' schools; and partly because the reunion of the fragmented Scottish Churches was now becoming a live issue, and Father's legal background and experience were much in demand at the Edinburgh headquarters of the Church of Scotland.

Our departure from Monzievaird was timed for midsummer as, in Mother's words, 'Hope had arisen that at Eastertide a longed-for daughter might be granted. And great was the delight to us both when on April 15th 1902, our daughter Helena was born, who became the apple of her father's eye.'

Now just a word about this 'apple' business. It is of course disheartening to be nobody's apple. Naturally the eldest son is Mother's Favourite Boy, and the youngest daughter Father's Little Lass, and anyone in between is just an ordinary run-o'-the-mill child. It doesn't help to be sour about it; so it seemed that the only thing to do was to compete as best one could, and never give up trying. But in the early years it was difficult for any of us to prevent some jealousy from creeping in. I have told how Teddy tried to poison me with red pepper. I fondly imagined my own record in this respect was clear; but Helena recently assured me that, when she was two, I tried to get rid of her by enticing her into the hall chest and sitting on the lid. Apparently my idea was that she would be eaten by earwigs, and disappear without trace. Vain hope! And really, now that I know her rather better than I did seventy years ago, I am not sorry that the plan miscarried. (Other things apart, it was Helena who years ago had devotedly assembled and typed our parents' memoir material which — gratefully — I have sometimes used.)

We were all sad to leave the Manse. I marked the occasion by falling out of the carriage, catching my coat on the bracket-step and being dragged along the road. My legs were a mess of dust and blood when we got to the doctor, but no bones were broken. Eventually, well bandaged, I climbed on to the box like a footman and sat beside MacGregor for our last ride to the station. MacGregor was rather upset and kept flicking the horse with his whip; whereupon Punch retaliated in the only way he could by slowly lifting his tail and venting his internal gases in our faces. He certainly had the best of it, as we were in no position to reply.

Farewell, dear Monzievaird!

Strathearn Lodge, a white three-storeyed villa, stands high on a ridge of ground at the west end of North Berwick. Only a narrow strip of golf-links lies between it and the beach. The view is arresting. Along the coast, a mile or two off shore, lies a string of fascinating islands: the Bass Rock, with its immense black cliffs and ever-circling sea-birds; green Craigleith, where the sheep go for summer grazing; the Lamb, its name belied by ferocious rocks; and mysterious Fidra, shaped like a great battleship at anchor close by the shore. Across the Firth of Forth on a clear day you see the rocky coast of the Kingdom of Fife, and away to the west Arthur's Seat, Edinburgh Castle, and the gaunt cantilevers of the Forth Bridge.

But North Berwick has a personality that appeals to a child's keen nose as well as to the eye. What's in the wind? The salt sea-spray, the tang of drying sea-weed, the fragrance of thyme and little flowers in the springy turf, and the warm smell of new-cut grass where old Smail has taken his leather-booted horse a-mowing along the fairways. And at closer quarters the exciting scent of a new golf-ball, and the less attractive but no less significant aroma of sandpaper and rust associated with the ritual of polishing iron clubs for the next day's play. Those irons by the way were not the standardised and numbered series of today, but individual weapons with names of a noble ancestry, the cleek, the mid-iron, jigger, mashie and niblick. As for golf-balls, we never had to buy them. The fourth hole of the Ladies' Links went past the front of the house, and enough drives were hooked over our wall to keep us well supplied.

Mother bought a bag of clubs and soon learned to play, though she was never a match for Father. On windy days her long skirts made it difficult for her to stand steadily at the ball, and when she hit it everyone ducked. At North Berwick the wind seemed to blow incessantly, and the result was usually described by Mother, who never swore, as 'quite exasperating'. So in time she became preoccupied with other things and her clubs were laid aside.

For Teddy, however, she arranged regular lessons from the best professionals. He had several from the great James Braid, that quiet, modest man who won the Open Championship four times in six years (a feat never likely to be repeated). After that he had regular coaching by the local pro, Ben Sayers, the little man with the long clubs whose memory enriches North Berwick golf to this day. Of course Teddy always outplayed me. Never having had any lessons I just copied him as best I could, and we played round the Ladies' Links amicably if not competitively.

Once after a good half-hour's ceaseless effort, I managed to chip my 'gutty' over a stone wall with Mother's flat-faced putter. She was so impressed that she gave me the club as a prize. I gradually helped myself to the others.

Robert Louis Stevenson, whose delicate health prejudiced him against the rough climate of his boyhood home, wrote of it thus:

> Edinburgh is liable to be beaten upon by all the winds that blow, to be drenched with rain, to be buried in cold sea fogs out of the east, and powdered with the snow as it comes flying southward from the Highland hills. The weather is raw and boisterous in winter, shifty and ungenial in summer, and a downright meteorological purgatory in the spring. The delicate die early, and I, as a survivor, among bleak winds and plumping rain, have been sometimes tempted to envy them their fate.

Written of course with tongue in cheek. North Berwick has the same boisterous and variable weather as Edinburgh; and there is no denying that the east wind, though bracing, exacts its price in coughs and colds of which we children had our share.

This soon led Mother to try on us her inherited veterinary or medical skill. For coughs we were given hot blackcurrant tea; and gruel, a concoction of pepper and salt with oatmeal, to make us perspire. For colds, our chests were rubbed with camphorated oil, we were given camphor pills, and lumps of sugar with eucalyptus drops, which were popular and probably effective. At night a Vapocresolene lamp on a bedside chair provided us with antiseptic fumes and the comforting presence of a night-light. Less obviously beneficial were those gritty 'grey powders', intended as a purge. Mother would pour the stuff from a thin paper envelope on to the tongue; but most of it, as soon as her back was turned, was regurgitated into a handkerchief. A harmless little deception surely, and done in self-defence; but when it came to countering deception Mother was more than equal to the occasion.

Her method in my case was to wake me from deep sleep with a whispered enticement. 'You've been a good boy today, so here is a treat for you.' Too sleepy to be suspicious I mumbled, 'What is it?' and was told 'a spoonful of syrup'. Grateful, if slightly surprised, I took it, and was told to suck the spoon clean. Then gradually the truth dawned; the syrup was there all right, but its real purpose was to glue into my teeth some gritty mess that I could well have done without. It was in fact our disgusting old friend Rhubarb-Bismuth-and-Soda; two tablets well grated up. Some years later, when being shown round Apsley House, I found that the Duke of Wellington had carried them in his field medicine-chest at Waterloo. Mother's grandfather of the 5th Dragoon Guards may have had a hand in that. But it seemed no reason why my inside should have had the same dosing as that of the Iron Duke. For a short period, in spite of my protests, mother's occasional night-time treats continued. They reached a climax when a wine-glass of 'nice orange-juice' was presented in which my lips soon detected the greasy touch of castor-oil. I am afraid I flung the contents against the wall, where it oozed hideously down, while I told Mother I could no longer trust her. That was the last of those under-cover dosings.

But there was one medicine which we children readily accepted, in spite of its outward resemblance to Syrup of Figs. It was Chlorodyne. When we were internally upset it soothed the tum and sent us to sleep, like gripe-water for a baby, only more so. But its accompanying literature rightly claimed more than that, and we read with enthusiasm of the wide range of diseases the Victorian age had to offer. 'Bronchitis, whooping-cough, colic and spasms' were mastered in no time; while 'fevers, ague, cholera, the plague, etcetera' might take a little longer. From a well-known History of the Boer War we get this glimpse: 'Gaunter and gaunter grew the soldiers of the Queen. Hunger and sickness played havoc with those fine regiments. But somehow the R.A.M.C. managed to patch the men up with *Chlorodyne* and quinine.' But most of all we liked the tableau conjured up by the testimonial from Edward (Excelsior!) Whymper, the celebrated Mountaineer: 'I always carry Chlorodyne on my travels, and have used it effectively on *others* on Mont Blanc.'

Father once said that if he were lost in the African Bush (a possibility we had overlooked) he would only need three remedies, Chlorodyne, gunpowder and whisky. When asked what the gunpowder was for, he explained that, if bitten by a snake, you put on the spot as much as will go on a shilling, and apply a lighted match. The whisky of course would be for bringing you round. He himself always took a modest dose at lunch-time and in the evening; but that, he said, was to ward off Evil Spirits.

In many ways life at Strathearn Lodge differed from life at Monzievaird Manse. For one thing we were no longer a Manse, and no one in trouble came seeking our help. We had stables, but no MacGregor, and no carriage; when necessary we hired a cab to go to the station. Our stables were never occupied, and only became a garage after we had gone. We had no cow; we kept no hens. Unknown to me we were moving into the twentieth century. But we still kept up the custom of family prayers. Every morning after breakfast, cook and both maids would file into the dining-room, each to their own special place. Mother or Nannie held Helena, and I sat on a footstool at Father's feet while he read the Bible. Usually the family read one verse and the servants the next, thus taking equal part. The idea may have been to remind ourselves that we would all be equal in the next world, if not in this one.

Mother recalled an incident when Father was reading the passage in Luke, Chapter 11, 'If a son shall ask bread of any of you that is a father, will he give him a stone?' At which Huntly turned quickly with an incredulous look and exclaimed, 'Oh, shoorly not!' They all laughed at that, as no doubt the disciples did at the time; but the mere idea that my Father would ever dream of tricking me was more than I could bear. I suppose, in a way, I thought of him as God.

Father was by now spending much of his time at the Church Headquarters in Edinburgh and, relying on Mother's initiative and drive, left her to decide all the more mundane affairs of the family, among them our education. Teddy was then aged eight, and Mother judged that he had outgrown the local girls' school. She therefore sent him to board at a preparatory school in Derbyshire. In retrospect it seems a surprising choice, but Mother had once met the Headmaster, a clergyman, during her visit to Grindelwald in 1897, and she did not hesitate in her choice. She rarely hesitated in any choice.

The Senior Headmistress of the North Berwick Girls' School had intimated that one Gordon son at a time was as much as the school could take. So when Teddy left she agreed without much enthusiasm that I could take his place; but her attitude softened when she found that I was less of a handful than my brother.

Life at school was less arduous than I had feared. My first attempt at recorded work was done on a slate. Some understanding person had attached a sponge, with which my scribblings and attempted caricatures could be quickly erased. In the hope of evoking any artistic talent that I might have inherited, they taught me to weave together strips of coloured paper, and to paint flowers having four yellow petals and a long green stalk. But no talent emerged. My real interest lay in the outside world, in gathering poppies, cornflowers and ox-eye daisies in the fields on the way to school. There was also a horse to feed through a gate and little wild strawberries to be found along the hedgerows. All this took time, anything from one to two hours in fact, though the distance was barely a mile. Unfortunately my Mistress did not believe the various reasons I gave for being late; so Mother put a small note-book in my satchel, in which entries were made in indelible ink:

Huntly left home   a.m.
Huntly reached school at   a.m.

Though thus humiliated, I yet managed to negotiate a fairly generous allowance of travelling time. Beyond that, I had no option but to submit to this first increase in the tempo of existence, a first hint of the rat-race in which I was later to be ruthlessly caught up, and about which so many people now complain. They have the sympathy of one who is once more free to look along the hedgerows for little wild strawberries.

About this time Mother and Father were often absent from home. Although they never told us, they were busy with the new house they were building on the southern outskirts of Edinburgh. This left only Nannie and the maids at home to look after me and baby Helena; so mother decided that to lighten their responsibility I should become a boarder at the school. I was given a small dressing-room next to the big bedroom which was shared by the two elderly sisters. One was the Headmistress (Teaching and Music), a stiff caustic lady with a grating voice; the other was the Headmistress (Feeding and General Conduct), a childless widow whose attitude to me was motherly and tolerant.

On Sundays they always lay in bed late; and I, impatient to get up, whiled away the time by singing to myself. The wall between our rooms was thin, and they must have found that my singing disturbed them; so, 'as a treat', I was taken into their bed at half past seven on condition I kept quite still. Too over-awed to move, I lay between them watching the flies on the ceiling. What a situation! The time passed so slowly that I took to praying that the bed might collapse; but nothing happened. At last in desperation I said, 'Excuse me', slid rapidly out of the bed, and went to the lavatory, where I remained until they got up. Next Sunday morning I kept very quiet and was relieved to find there was no further mention of bed-sharing. All of which reinforced my feeling that when grown-ups propose something 'as a treat', it was a time to be on one's guard.

My only other memory of that school was our long walk through the town to Church on Sunday, when I formed the tail end of the girls' crocodile, and had to endure the occasional banter of boys in the street without replying. The Parish Church was a modern building which to me had an uncanny atmosphere. It probably acquired this from the High Church nearby, now a centuries-old ruin in which, so legend had it, Old Nick himself had once appeared in human guise and delivered a sermon which terrified the congregation. That the preacher really was His Infernal Majesty had been established beyond all doubt by the strong smell of brimstone as he whirled down the pulpit stairs and vanished through the vestry.

In order to preserve my home ties and provide me with suitable exercise, the Headmistresses sent me for afternoon walks with Helena and her Nannie. As we never met any-one, these excursions were boring beyond belief. The empty road from North Berwick ran as straight as a ruler through open empty fields towards the next village of Dirleton, which was out of sight. The fences bordering the road, the telegraph wires, the single footpath, all met as straight lines in a single vanishing point. One might walk at our speed for half an hour and the prospect was still the same — infinity. Nowadays if I go for a walk, I like to know where I am going, how far it is, how long it will take, what we shall find when we get there, and whether we should turn back. On our Dirleton walks, these ques-tions could have no answer; we never saw Dirleton, and it was only in later years that I found the place really existed.

With our minds thus fixed on Eternity we would daunder along the road, Helena comfortably ensconced in her well-upholstered pram and watching me with a benevolent and slightly patronising air, as much as to say, 'You see, I am *propelled*.' Nannie it was who made these walks bearable, by sharing with me some of the wisdom she had absorbed in her own youth. It was thus that I learned that if you put on a stocking inside out, it's bad luck to turn it right way round; crossed knives mean a quarrel; if you see lightning flash you must cover all mirrors; little girls must never be said to have 'red' hair, always 'auburn', or you hurt their Nannie's feelings; the evil influence of a hare can be warded off by keeping your fingers crossed till you see a white dog; when people come to tea, it's smarter to have 'boughten' cakes than home-made; in a tea-shop you must always drink from your cup left-handed; foxgloves are deadly poison; and if you get a scratch on the skin between thumb and fore-finger you die of lock-jaw, in agony. There seemed no end to her fund of useful information.

But though we never met anyone on those walks, we once found ourselves being followed. It was in the short piece of road still called Strathearn Road, and we were nearly home, when we became aware of a drunken tramp staggering after us. Between him and us there was a freshly-laid piece of roadway, very rough and newly sprayed with tar, waiting for the steam-roller. On this the tramp tripped, falling flat on his face, which made me laugh. But when he rose unsteadily to his feet he was a fearful sight. His hands and front were smeared with sticky tar, and blood was running down his tarry face. He shouted at us as if it was all our fault, and then came staggering towards us to take his revenge.

Realising that this was a situation in which the family motto had best be forgotten, I urged Nannie into a run, closed and bolted the main gate, then locked the front door and called to the maids to prepare the house for the coming attack. When the tramp reached our outer gate he shook it furiously, but his clumsy hands could not turn the key from inside. Presently we saw him go back and vent his anger on the driver of the steam-roller, and realised with relief that the enemy was repulsed and the battle won.

7

Drumearn

In the summer of 1903 King Edward VII and Queen Alexandra came to the Scottish capital and held Court at the Palace of Holyrood House. Mother had not been presented before and probably she was secretly longing for the opportunity. Her account fifty years later so artlessly reflects the regal atmosphere of the occasion that I give it practically verbatim:

When the Court announcement appeared in the 'Scotsman', my husband expressed the wish that I should be presented, though at first I hardly saw the necessity[!]. But knowing Lord and Lady Balfour of Burleigh well, he asked her if she would be so kind as to sponsor me, and to this she graciously agreed. The order was 'Afternoon dress and toques', so I had to think up something.

I had a lovely piece of pale green georgette painted with lilies of the valley by one of my girlhood's friends, and I thought of using it as a deep collar and having a light champagne-coloured dress in a silky material which would set it off. Then a pretty champagne toque with a spray of lilies of the valley on the side, and a bouquet of lilies with a few little pink roses among them made a very attractive ensemble. When I went afterwards to the chief Edinburgh photographer, I remember he complimented me on such a well thought-out design.

It was rather an ordeal passing the presence, and their Majesties looked absolutely bored and never smiled at anyone. The stalwart members of the Royal Archers, in their picturesque uniform with Tam-o'-shanter and long eagle's feather, standing in each window niche in the long corridors leading to the Throne Room made an impressive picture. Later we met various friends in the grounds and were regaled with ices and light refreshments in the tents before making our departure. I was pleased with the experience when it was all over.

That autumn we moved into our new house, Drumearn, the back garden of which looked south across the Hermitage Valley at the Braid Hills. It was a fine three-storeyed house in red sandstone in the Georgian style. There was a big expanse of grey granite gravel for carriages in front of the house; and many were the happy half-hours I spent raking out the wheel marks for a penny, a useful addition to my weekly pocket money of fourpence.

Mother and Father had had fun over the details of the design, as we found on our arrival. The main entrance was reminiscent of the barbican outwork of a castle. Carved on the great lintel-stone over the doorway was a monogram of the initials O & A G, intertwined with a wreath of ivy, the Gordon Emblem of Constancy, doubly appropriate to Mother's maiden name. Below was carved the inscription, *Pax Intrantibus, Salus Exeuntibus*. From the entrance lobby you passed into a large two-storeyed hall, off which was Father's study, a big room lined with books, awesome but mostly dull; a dining-room with a boar's head carved in stone over the fireplace; and a morning-room, thrillingly equipped with a telephone on the wall. Our new number was only 1892, because there were few of these machines in Edinburgh at that time.

A somewhat similar innovation was the speaking-tube, of which the lower end was in the kitchen passage, and the upper end on the top floor, where the servants' rooms were. The intention was to save them having to run up and down stairs. Each mouth-piece had a wooden whistle, like a cork in a bottle; so if you wanted to speak to Agnes in the afternoon you took out the whistle on the ground floor, and blew hard into the tube. If you were lucky you might hear the other whistle sound faintly at the top of the house. When Agnes had reached the top-floor mouth-piece, she might say 'hullo', and start listening. Or she might blow back, so that you got a puff in the ear, which tickled; or more probably you both started talking into the mouthpiece at the same time which got you nowhere; or in despair you ended up blowing the whistles at each other, which was equally futile. In fact, we found that apart from the first loud blow, signalling 'You are wanted', the system was quite maddening.

More effective was the system for opening the solid wooden back door of our street entrance. This was modelled on the ancient procedure for opening a castle draw-bridge. The caller would pull a brass handle beside the door, from which a chain running through an underground pipe caused a bell to jangle in the kitchen. Whoever was in the kitchen then pulled up a handle attached to another underground chain which set the pavement door ajar. The caller entered and the outer door would close behind him with a click. While he walked up the path through the vegetable garden to the house, the cook could see whether it was a friendly tradesman on his delivery round. If Drumearn had been fully equipped as a castle, she could probably have arranged that, if the visitor was unwelcome, a consignment of boiling oil or molten lead would descend on his head. As it was, the procedure was still useful in preventing enterprising strangers from helping themselves to our vegetables.

The best room in the house was the drawing-room at the top of the front stairs. It was a large white room, with a domed ceiling embossed with boars' heads, angels' heads and occasional sprays of ivy. The walls were of white watered silk. Framed in apple-green curtains the bow windows gave a glorious view of the Braid Hills. To one side, with the light shining on its keyboard, stood Mother's Steinway Boudoir Grand, tastefully draped with a silk shawl, and decorated with family photographs. As we children only entered the room on special occasions, it was always spotless and smelt sweetly of potpourri and flowers.

On the first floor were also the five family bedrooms and a large spare room. The cook and two resident maids each had a comfortable bed-sitting-room on the top floor with the best views of all over Edinburgh and the Firth of Forth. There was a bathroom on each floor, but ordinary washing was still done with basin and ewer in the bedrooms. Each morning the housemaid brought in a can of hot water, pulled back the curtains with a rattle of curtain-rings, and announced the time and the state of the weather. The whole house was electrically lit, and gas fires had been fitted in the bedrooms more for speed and convenience than from any pressing need to save labour. Mother was a considerate mistress, and the domestic staff seemed happy and contented. Drumearn was indeed a lovely home, in which there was every encouragement for a young family to grow up like the angels so thoughtfully portrayed on the drawing-room ceiling.

When we moved to Drumearn Mother was about thirty-three. She was a bonny woman of medium height and held herself well; she was plump without being fat, and had a pleasant jolly face with good features and the Grecian profile so much admired in Edwardian times. Her brown hair, lightly curled round her forehead, was brushed up at the back and coiled on the crown of her head. On this secure pad various types of hat were transfixed with ornate hat-pins of lethal length. But in the evening she let her hair down and loved to brush its full glossy length before going to bed. She usually dressed with quiet good taste, especially when appearing as the Minister's Wife. But sometimes, when on her own, she indulged in bright colours.

Mother had a great store of energy, and was busy all day long; running the household, keeping a close eye on the cook; making and repairing clothes for her children; seeing to the flowers; keeping accounts in great detail; often out shopping. She was good at anything with her hands: lace-making; playing the piano, though she had no time for practising now; painting anything from a bathroom to a heron on a silk screen, or landscapes in water-colours. Pinned to her blouse over her heart she wore a small gold watch which she frequently consulted in the vain effort to make us all punctual.

She read us many stories of all kinds; and poetry too, usually dramatic, such as this from Robert Browning, her favourite poet:

> 'You're wounded!' 'Nay,' the soldier's pride
> Touched to the quick, he said :
> 'I'm killed, Sire!' And his chief beside
> Smiling the boy fell dead.

(We enjoyed acting that last line with suitable panache.) And that other rollicking piece, 'How they brought the Good News from Aix to Ghent', or vice versa:

> I sprang to the stirrup, and Joris, and he;
> I galloped, Dirck galloped, we galloped all three.

Stirring action was what Mother liked, with a good bit of sentiment thrown in; and sometimes the sentiment was overpowering. Like many grown-ups Mother did not seem to realise how indelible was the impact made on the impressionable minds of young children by pathetic or gruesome stories told with great feeling by their own parents. I cannot to this day read Hans Andersen's story of 'The Little Match Girl' without dissolving into tears. The stories of those well-named Germans, the Brothers Grimm, filled our sleeping hours with horrid imaginings, so that Teddy used to wake screaming and take refuge in Mother's bed, and even placid Helena took to sleep-walking down the back stairs. It was perhaps significant that I did not seek protection in Mother's bed but kept my fears to myself, which possibly made them worse; it certainly produced sweating, shuddering and sometimes even vomiting.

On Sunday evenings, being thought of as the musical one, I had to join Mother in hymn-singing at the harmonium, because it would have hurt her to refuse. Some of the hymns I liked: 'There is a happy land', 'Jesus loves me, This I know', and especially 'Holy, Holy, Holy', portraying that Celestial Ice-Rink where all the saints were triumphantly 'casting down their golden crowns around the glassy sea; Cherubim and Seraphim falling down before Thee', a truly joyful knockabout scene. But other hymns alerted my super-sensitive fears: why were 'angels watching round my bed'? Wolves, perhaps! And there was one hymn in particular that I found quite terrifying, especially as sung dramatically by Mother, with organ-stops pulled out for increased effect. It was about the Lost Sheep. To a tune full of foreboding, it starts with one of the most ominous couplets I know,

> There were ninety and nine that safely lay
>> In the shelter of the fold;
> But one was out on the hills away, [me, of course!]
>> Far off from the gates of gold;
> Away on the mountains wild and bare,
>> Away from the tender Shepherd's care.

Rejecting the suggestion that ninety-nine sheep were enough, the tender Shepherd sets out in the darkness and through deep rivers on his loving search, till

Out in the desert He heard its cry,
    Sick and helpless and ready to die.

'Lord, whence are those blood-drops all the way,
    That mark out the mountain's track?
Lord whence are Thy hands so rent and torn?'
    'They are pierced tonight by many a thorn.'

And all through the mountains, thunder-riven,   [what a line!]
    And up from the rocky steep,
There rose a cry to the gate of Heaven,
    'Rejoice, I have found My sheep.'

This triumphant ending (fortissimo!) left me emotionally battered, though Mother no doubt recognised in my flushed face the first signs of religious enthusiasm. Speaking as a lost sheep, my own feeling was that it would have been better had I been left quietly to expire in the desert. The author of the hymn, Elizabeth Cecilia Clephane (1830–69), can little know in her tortured heaven what I owe to her and Mother, namely, a life-long phobia which requires me, when in church, to sit as near as possible to the exit. Strangely enough (or is it?) that hymn has never been announced in my hearing. If it had, I and possibly others would have been out of the door like bolting rabbits.

But Mother had too lively a sense of humour to be fanatically religious. She just lived her life trusting in the goodness of God, and convinced that her own Guardian Angel would see to the details. She was very good company among all sorts of people, and her skill in mimicry made her an amusing story-teller. To emphasise any point she often used her hands in gesture, as her French Huguenot ancestors must have done.

Now for Father. By this time he was nearing fifty, which was a good deal older in those days than it is now. He was of average height, slim, with a soldierly bearing and cropped ginger moustache which pricked when he kissed you. His forehead was high, and his thin fair hair was well brushed back and held in place with 'Pomade' from the Army & Navy Stores. The special feature of his face was the kind expression in his blue eyes. I cannot recall that he was ever angry with us, though he may often have had reason to be. He certainly never lost his temper and never raised his voice. But his tenderness towards us was no sign of lack of spirit. At hypocritical behaviour he would grow hot with indignation; and two-faced politicians he would denounce as 'rascals', with a vehemence that surely must have made their ears tingle and sometimes drew a mild remonstrance from Mother.

His sense of humour was equally sharp; and some of his stories, told in a variety of broad Scottish accents, were really funny, and moved him to such laughter that he had to wipe the tears from his cheeks before he could finish them. By contrast his manner in the pulpit probably owed much to Lord Gordon. He was quiet, transparently sincere, and preached the Gospel more as a lawyer stating a convincing case than by an easy appeal to the emotions.

Except when he wore tweeds on holiday, his dress never varied. His trousers, long frock coat and waistcoat were of black Vicuna cloth of the finest quality, which, surmounted by his clerical (or dog) collar, and soft flat clerical hat, constituted a uniform which set him apart from the rest of us. After a rather silent breakfast he would take the *Scotsman* and disappear into his study, where he stayed deep in the paper and smoking Turkish cigarettes. Their brand, as he never tired of telling us, was Ayah Solouk, 'grown on the site of Ancient Ephesus'. Father may have felt that this tobacco, drawn from the very soil trodden by the redoubtable St Paul, in the place where he had faced Demetrius the Silversmith and his ferocious supporters, shouting by the hour for Diana of the Ephesians, might give him 'that little something the others haven't got'. At any rate the corner of the room where he sat in his leather armchair was fragrant with clouds of Pauline incense until about ten o'clock in the morning. Then he would mutter

'Time to be off', blow the stub out of his cherry-wood cigarette holder, brush the ash off his waistcoat, don coat and hat, kiss Mother goodbye, and with a brisk step set out for the Morningside tram that would carry him down town to the Church of Scotland Headquarters.

For our entertainment, as each of us reached the age of four or five, Father would read us extracts from an Anthology of Humorous Verse, some of which had been well received at the Manse soirées at Monzievaird. But like many other grown-ups of that time he assumed that anything entertaining to grown-ups (and that included mock-horror situations) would be equally laughable to young children. The verses he read and re-read included 'John Gilpin' and 'The Laird of Cockpen' which I found odd but laughable. But Anstey's 'Burglar Bill' puzzled this five-year-old, because I had never thought of armed burglars as amusing; and when Baby Bella reached her climax with

> 'Sank 'oo, Misser Burglar, sank 'oo!
> And, betause 'oo's been so nice,
> See what I have dot — a tartlet!
> Gweat big gweedies ate the ice.'

it all seemed so idiotic that my reaction was one of stunned silence.

Then there was 'Little Billee', by William Makepeace Thackeray. It was a story in verse of three sailors, who found themselves at sea in a boat with their food all gone.

> To gorging Jack says guzzling Jimmy
> 'We've nothing left, us must eat we.' . . .

> 'Oh! Billy, we're going to kill and eat you
> So undo the button of your chemie.'
> 'Make haste, make haste,' says guzzling Jimmy.
> While Jack pulled out his snickersnee.
> [Next moment they see the British Navy, with Admiral Napier,
> K.C.B.]

So when they got aboard of the Admiral's,
He hanged fat Jack and flogged Jimmie;
But as for little Bill he made him
The Captain of a Seventy-three.

Not only was I repelled by all this, but I was quite at a loss as to why my own father thought it funny. For his sake I produced an uneasy smile; but soon slid off his knee and found something else to do. Taking it literally, as I was left to do, such sadistic humour provided material for nightmares over several years. But when at the age of ten or thereabouts I began to recognise it for the depraved rubbish it was, my mind discarded it in favour of more convincing children's verse, such as 'The Wreck of the Hesperus', which I soon had to memorise at school.

One last horror I beg leave to inflict on the reader, because it has some significance in being the fount and origin of the worst fear that beset us as children, namely the fear of wolves. It seems fair to assume that one is not haunted by stories with happy endings. Therefore I pass over that vague tale of the Russian horse-sleigh being overtaken by a pack of wolves and the driver throwing overboard bits of food, fur-coats and possibly his best friend to distract their attention; until with no friends and only one horse left, he reaches the safety of the village in the nick of time. That seems a fairly happy ending, at least by Russian standards. So that did not worry us unduly.

Then there was Little Red Riding Hood — rather more suspect. According to Andrew Lang's *Blue Fairy Book*, which I think Father used, the wolf arriving in advance at the grandmother's cottage, 'ate her up in a moment', and then donning her clothes got into bed. When Little Red Riding Hood arrived and had finished her traditional cross-talk with, 'Grandmamma, what great teeth you have got', the wicked wolf 'fell upon her and ate her all up'. That is Andrew Lang's ending, and one cannot call it a happy one. Mother, however, saved the situation by insisting that just as the wicked wolf was about to eat the little girl, a wood-cutter entered and with one swipe of his axe, cut off the wolf's head; whereupon out popped the grandmother who had not yet been digested by the wolf, and all three of them sat down to a jolly spread from the goodies in the little girl's basket. Thus the wicked wolf met a well-deserved end, and that story no longer had power to haunt us.

But now comes 'Beth-gelert', a true Welsh story of the thirteenth century, reaching a high level of sheer savagery. The poem tells how Prince Llewelyn when out deer-hunting with his friends noticed that his deer-hound Gelert, usually the first in the field, 'so true, so brave — a lamb at home, a lion in the chase', was no longer with them. The hunting over, Llewelyn returned home angry and uneasy because of his infant son who had been left in his cot:

> But when he gained his castle-door
>   Aghast the chieftain stood;
> The hound all o'er was smeared with gore;
>   His lips, his fangs, ran blood.
> [Hastening into his chamber]
> O'erturned his infant's bed he found,
>   With blood-stained covert rent;
> And all around, the walls and ground
>   With recent blood besprent.
> He called his child — no voice replied —
>   He searched with terror wild;
> Blood, blood he found on every side,
>   But nowhere found his child.
> 'Hell-hound! my child's by thee devoured',
>   The frantic father cried;
> And to the hilt his vengeful sword
>   He plunged in Gelert's side.

Poor Gelert's dying yell was answered from beneath a tumbled heap by an infant's cry. And there at last Llewelyn found his son!

> Nor scathe had he, nor harm, nor dread;
>> But, the same couch beneath,
> Lay a gaunt wolf, all torn and dead,
>> Tremendous still in death. . . .
> His gallant hound the wolf had slain
>> To save Llewelyn's heir!

Father's dramatic rendering conveyed more horror than he realised, and by this time my hair was standing on end. The dreadful scene might so easily be repeated any day. The frantic father, not there when most wanted; the gaunt, tremendous wolf, bloody fangs and all; the child indeed, but this time with no gallant deerhound to defend him; no, not so much as a Pekinese! The impressionable mind was aghast.

What an indescribable relief it was when Mother produced those Beatrix Potter books and, leaving behind the morbid horrors of Celtic Legend, we entered the sunlit gardens where Peter Rabbit stole his first lettuce under the nose of Mr McGregor.

Beyond the door of our drawing-room at Drumearn was a passage leading to the bedrooms, a dark passage, made darker by a curtain hung across the entry. When Helena was old enough to become aware of such dangers, she was certain that behind the curtain there lurked a pack of wolves. By that time I was nearly immune to childish fears. A pack was too much. One gaunt wolf, possibly; though now dead, and only fit to be kicked aside. Yet to this very day, if Helena and I returned, behind the curtain there would still be waiting for us a ghostly *Something*.

8
Montreux and Merchiston

When Teddy returned from his Derbyshire preparatory school for the Christmas holidays, it was noticed that he had a hard persistent cough, and the doctor was sent for. Dr Carter was the perfect family physician. One heard the grinding of his carriage wheels on the gravel, and when he entered the bedroom and looked at you with his friendly smile you felt at once that all would be well. A slim erect man, clean-shaven, with blue eyes and a crop of iron-grey hair, he was always immaculately dressed in a black frock-coat, well-creased grey-striped trousers, a grey double-breasted waistcoat, and a silver-grey tie. And with him a faint aura of scented soap.

'Well, Huntly,' he would say in his quiet resonant voice, 'what's the trouble?' Then followed his examination, apparently casual, of throat, temperature, pulse, feeling for swollen glands, all masked by a running question and answer about your games, your school, and your other interests. Next from his top hat the stethoscope was produced, made of oak and shaped like a very thin candlestick; the narrow end was applied to your chest, the wide base to his ear. After all that, the diagnosis, with the comment, 'There's a lot of it about' (so that your trouble was by now only a drop in the ocean among all the others) and finally the prescription which he would drop off at the chemist to be delivered to us by the chemist's boy within the hour. Lastly the pat on the shoulder, the friendly smile as he left you, the reassuring word with Mother as they went down the stairs, and once more the sound of carriage wheels on the gravel. Usually the patient, who previously may have been feeling rather sorry for himself, would by now be shouting, 'Can I get up now?'

But this time Dr Carter's examination of Teddy took longer than usual. Pleurisy was mentioned, and with tuberculosis at that time a widespread and killing disease, a specialist was called in. He confirmed the beginning of T.B. in one lung, and advised that Teddy should be sent to a sanatorium in the Highlands. Knowing the Highland weather only too well, Father was against this and said he would take him to Switzerland. Mother's chief determination was that he should never return to that awful school in Derbyshire where he had evidently contracted the disease. So off they went, accompanied by Father's great friend Dr Playfair of St Andrews, in search of health among the Italian Lakes, St Moritz and Pontresina, leaving Mother and me (aged six) and Helena (aged two) at Drumearn.

To our great relief Teddy was pronounced cured within a few months, and it was decided that they should spend a year out there to make quite certain there was no recurrence. We were to join them in the autumn, and Drumearn would be let for the winter to meet the cost of these foreign junketings.

Meanwhile Mother looked round for a school for me in our suburb of Morningside, and decided on Lady Margaret's, another girls' school. Perhaps her faith in boys' schools had been shaken by the Derbyshire one, and she felt I would somehow be safer at girls' schools, as she knew something about them. Being the only small boy there I was of course mothered by the mistresses and older girls, and made some quite exciting friends among the younger ones. I did very little work as I only attended in the mornings. My favourite activity was 'fan-dancing'. This, I should perhaps explain, had not yet developed into its modern forms, but only consisted in graceful rhythmic movements with a fan. We also waved gossamer scarves in the air, in a way reminiscent of the Dance of the Seven Veils by which Salome got her own back on St John the Baptist; though her musical accompaniment must have been rather more seductive than that thumped out on our school piano.

In the afternoons I had private tuition by a governess because my reading was at least a year behind Teddy's at the same age. I was barely emerging from the 'C—A—T spells CAT' stage, and could not possibly read the 23rd Psalm. On my fifth birthday Father gave me a Pictorial New Testament on the flyleaf of which he had written in his beautiful flowing handwriting my name, and 'presented on his 5th Birthday'. He was pretending I came up to the standard of Gordon sons, and with typical kindness spared me the test.

Mother, always anxious to do the best for her children and accepting that I was scholastically rather dim, looking around for something I might be less dim at, thought she detected some signs of musical promise. Alas, it was only her wishful thinking. However, she engaged an elderly spinster with breast-plate corsage and protruding eyes to teach me the piano. But the mental process by which I translated a note on the music page into a letter of the alphabet, and thence to an ivory key on the piano, remained a laborious one. My teacher was terribly frustrated at my slow-motion rendering of 'The Merry Peasant', and kept hitting me over the knuckles with a pencil. She might have been surprised to know that her opinion of me as a pupil was matched by mine of her as a teacher. We were all glad when our preparation for the journey to Switzerland brought those time-wasting lessons to an end. At least they had established beyond all doubt that Mother had not produced another infant Handel.

After our train journey from Edinburgh, the Channel crossing, and a night in a French train, we all felt rather dazed as we stepped out on the platform at Montreux, on the lake of Geneva. Father was nowhere to be seen, but at last we spotted Teddy, accompanied by a strange figure. This person wore a brown tweed knickerbocker suit, leather leggings with spiral straps, a small tweed cap, and flowing blue tie. The face was covered by a pointed auburn beard, through which shone a pair of smiling blue eyes. Father! The reunion was a wildly happy one, but shocking. That Father should thus abandon his normal clerical dress for tweeds was one thing. But that his face should now look so unmistakably Christ-like was really too much of a good thing. Mother would have none of it. Years afterwards she wrote:

> He looked more like a sailor than a clergyman, and I did not appreciate the change. However, after a visit to a Swiss hairdresser, he appeared with his moustache and a little goatee beard. After a short time this also disappeared, and Arthur Gordon was once more the nice-looking man I had married.

Father had had his fling!

Teddy and I were sent to school, a school where not a word of English was spoken. My brother was by now pretty fluent. For me it was, 'Fermez la porte, s'il vous plaît.' Gibberish. I would open the window. Loud laughter from the other pupils. In despair, I closed the door. Applause. That way I soon learned. We were there for six months. By that time, after a bad dream I would wake up protesting to Mother in fluent French.

Everyone had to learn something. Even Helena's nurse began to take French lessons. Mother did more water-colour painting and learnt to play the organ. 'But I found it needed so much brain for reading the music, attending to one's hands and feet, and stops at the sides to draw out, that I felt it was beyond me.' She once consented to stand in for the organist at a funeral. 'I was rather flummoxed when it came to the retiring voluntary. I prayed that the exit with the coffin would be fairly rapid as I could only play the beginning of it; but the undertakers were very slow in getting away, and I gave up in despair before the cortege disappeared, and felt very ashamed at my perform-ance!'

When Teddy and I went together to school our High-land dress came in for much comment. On our second day we found a line of boys obstructing the roadway with linked arms and jeering at us, 'Des robes! Des robes!' Realising instinctively the effectiveness of a hard thrust against an extended line, Teddy shouted, 'Scotland for ever!' and we went at them with heads down and fists flying. The breakthrough was decisive and we were not baited again.

Our way to school led through a vineyard path, and past a slaughterhouse. A piece of wood missing from a high boundary fence enabled us to see what was going on. It was fascinating to see a man get astride a squealing pig and, with a quick upward movement of his hand, cut its throat and hold it while the blood poured into a steaming bowl, until quickly the squealing died away and the animal collapsed. It was something to boast about at school. It never gave me any nightmares. I can't think why. Perhaps I was getting tough.

Another incident of that time is imprinted on my memory, and, I think a little unhappily, on Mother's too. For some time she had noticed that when asked a question I usually replied, 'What?' and had to have it repeated. This she had put down to my slow-wittedness. But she now recognised it as a deafness so bad that she took me to an ear-nose-and-throat specialist in Lausanne to see what could be done. He took one look at the back of my throat, took Mother outside and told her my adenoids should be removed. He offered to do it there and then. Mother believed that when something unpleasant was to happen the person affected should never be told in advance. *She* knew, and that was enough. She just told me the nice Swiss doctor was going to improve my deafness.

The doctor patted me on the head, installed me in a dentist's chair and swathed me in a white sheet. He then asked if I was comfortable, a strange inquiry. A reassurance from Mother that 'You'll be quite all right' confirmed my worst suspicions. Fearfully I gripped the chair while a leather strap was fastened round my chest and arms. My mouth was gagged open. There was a prolonged business with mirrors and lights and swabbing of my throat, conducted in silence. Then, still without any explanation, a powerful nurse gripped my head from behind, while the nice doctor passed instruments into the back of my mouth and began to remove lumps of flesh with a rending sound. It did not hurt a lot because my throat had been cocained, but it frightened me out of my wits to see the bloody gobbets brought out and put into a dish under my nose.

Mother recorded this performance with masterly under-statement:

> The doctor asked me to hold the child's head steady whilst he applied the guillotine. This was more than I had the nerve to do; so a nurse was called in, and in a moment it was done on one side, and we returned by train to Montreux. Alas, a second visit was necessary and, if I remember aright, not quite so easy, as 'once bit, twice shy.'

Yes, Mother dear, you do remember aright. The policy of secrecy was now split wide open. The ensuing week passed about as cheerfully as if I were a criminal awaiting execution; for at the age of seven, imagination is apt to magnify such ordeals a hundredfold. And when once more the electric train carried me along the shores of the lake of Geneva, it was with difficulty that I controlled my mounting terror. I counted off the telegraph poles as we neared that dreaded consulting-room. Again the hideous performance was carried through, just to tidy up a few loose ends. It took quite a time as the Swiss are very tidy people. However the result was undeniably good. I could at last hear normally. My slow-wittedness soon began to disappear. And I had a new parlour trick; the tea that I drank ran out of my nose.

It was not until many years later, middle life in fact, that it dawned on me that my life-long aversion to train journeys was traceable to this early experience. But by then there was no shifting it. That rather unintelligent being who operates out of sight 'in the subconscious' had got things irretrievably mixed up. Ridiculous though it may seem, I am still uneasy when travelling alone in a train, though I enjoy it in the company of friends. My own children accepted anaesthetics (but that's almost cheating!) and operations with very little fear, having had a full explanation in advance.

It comforts me to think that I am not alone in suffering unreasonable fears. Helena recently told me that as a small child she was once feeding corn to some hens when a half-tame jackdaw swooped down and started pecking at the shiny buttons on her boots. Terrified, she ran round and round the yard with the big black bird pecking at her ankles, while the grown-ups watching her roared with laughter. As a result, throughout her life she has been unable even to touch a chicken, or indeed any feathered creature — except, of course, with knife and fork.

On our return to Scotland, my brother and I started our real education as day-boys at Merchiston Castle Preparatory School, which was a short walk and tram-ride from our home. My fluent French enabled me to skip French 'prep' without retribution. Apart from that our French classes were a joy because of our unique French master. A lanky spectacled Scot, known as 'Old Connie', he had the gift of doing lightning comic sketches on the blackboard which kept us in fits of laughter, and on tip-toe to see what he would draw next. We all had to comment, and as our conversation had to be conducted only in French we learned the language almost without being aware of it.

Much of our general learning was by heart. 'The Charge of the Light Brigade', 'The Inchcape Rock'; 'Lucy Gray'; 'Scots Wha Hae'; 'Wee sleekit, cow'rin, tim'rous beastie'; and passages from Shakespeare; easily learnt at that age and never forgotten. And of course, the Sermon on the Mount, and 13th Corinthians, and other famous passages; a new verse every day. Morning Prayers for the whole school were taken by the Headmaster, and while he read the prayer that we should 'fall into no sin, neither run into any kind of danger' most of us were feverishly memorising the new verse for the day, and praying 'not me today, Lord; not me today'. When the accumulated danger of un-learnt verses became too great, one just had to concentrate and learn the whole lot at one go.

No one can memorise chapters of the New Testament without absorbing something of the teaching too. Thus when on a wintry day a wretched-looking tramp came to our front door asking pathetically for some food or cast-off clothing, up came the injunction, 'He that hath two coats, let him impart to him that hath none'; so I gladly imparted to him Father's new overcoat, and called to the cook to bring some food. By the time she reached the front door the tramp had disappeared, and what I had delighted in as a Christian act (infrequent for me) only brought down on my head a shower of abuse. I felt deeply wronged, and in a righteous fury retaliated with a gesture of the foot which caught the cook's shin with such force and accuracy that she sank stricken to the ground.

What Father or Mother thought of all this was never explained to me, and as I was not looking for trouble I did
not inquire.

Morningside was a socially well-to-do suburb, and normally one saw no sign of poverty in our part of Edinburgh.
A body called the Charity Organisation Society existed to
channel help to 'the deserving poor' and prevent kind-
hearted residents from being exploited by professional
tramps. We subscribed annually to it. When a deserving
case called and asked us for help, Father or Mother would
sign their name on a pink card and hand it to the appli-
cant who (if genuine) could then report at some address
in central Edinburgh and be given some form of help that
might match his need. It seemed a sensible arrangement,
though terribly impersonal. It can hardly be denied that at
a time when the normal wage was only 20s. to 30s. a week
(though a penny could then buy a fruit bun or a glass of
milk), there probably was real poverty in parts of Edinburgh.
But we never saw it, and the Press rarely mentioned it.
The following extract from *Edwardian Parade* by James
Laver gives a fairly true picture of the prevailing situation:

> I can remember my mother helping to serve soup, which could be
> bought by the needy for a penny a jug. . . . Neither the tradesmen
> who provided the materials for the soup, nor those ladies who
> served it, appeared to think it wrong that in a rich country fami-
> lies could be in such want that they would queue with jugs for a
> pennyworth of soup. There was nothing wrong with the people of
> that date, they were just as kind-hearted and easily moved as we
> are today; it was the way they thought that was different;
> poverty was something that happened — just as some people were
> born cripples; you helped, but you did not expect to cure them
> — indeed there were many who supposed it would be upsetting
> God's purpose if you did.

My own Mother used to visit and subscribe to a Home

for Crippled Children in Marchmont Road. She once took me there, an embarrassing experience. I was very sorry for the children, but they seemed comfortable and contented and not at all depressed at being crippled; and I could see no way to help them. But neither Mother nor I could believe that somehow Jesus, who loved the little children (or his more remote Father) could possibly have inflicted this life-long handicap on them. That just could not be true.

Merchiston Castle in the late sixteenth century had been the home of John Napier, whose name is widely execrated among schoolboys as the Inventor of Logarithms. He also had a more interesting reputation locally as a Wizard. On an occasion when something valuable had been stolen from the Castle, Napier made his servants pass in turn through his study and stroke the back of a black cock, known to be his familiar spirit; the inference was that the cock would crow when touched by the thief. The cock did not crow, but the thief was identified as the only one whose hand was not blackened by the soot which Napier had spread on the cock's back.

On another occasion the Wizard was annoyed by a neighbour, whose pigeons kept eating the grain from the stooks of corn drying in the Castle fields. He threatened to impound them. The neighbour defiantly replied that he would first have to catch them. Next day the pigeons were seen to be staggering about in the fields, and the Wizard duly collected them for his larder.

Living at a time of threatened Spanish invasion, Napier invented 'a round chariot of mettle made of the proofs of double muskett, to breake the array of the enemies battle'; and some 'devises of sayling under the water', as well as 'other devises and stratagemes for harming of the enemyes by the grace of God'.

In more modern times the Castle and its grounds were converted for use as a public school, and a number of houses beside it in Colinton Road were used as the Preparatory School. When we returned to the Prep, Teddy being one of the older boys became a boarder; while I being not yet eight continued as a day-boy. Boarders were rarely allowed out even at weekends, and their only chance of buying sweets during the week was when a confectioner brought in a basket on Wednesday evenings, from which they could buy not more than four pen'orth each. The situation was thus all set for a black market in which Teddy held the controlling position, while I was to do the work and take the risks.

The plan was that once or twice every week when on my way home I was to make the required purchases at the shops, return and call in at the Masters' Common Room to ask the necessary permission to re-enter the School and get a book which I had left behind. Teddy would then relieve me of my purchases, refunding the money, and I would finally make off for the Braid Hills tram-car and home.

As a black market it was a failure because we were all too honest with each other. I played my part because I was sorry for Ted's toffee-starved friends, but would take neither money nor favours from them. Admittedly there was a thrill in returning with my overcoat pockets full of sweets and asking the master on duty for permission to get a book. Once or twice it was touch and go whether or not I was searched; but suspicions were lulled because I had an honest face. After a time, too, Teddy's friends had prickings of conscience over the risks I was taking for their sake without reward. They sought to pay me in cash or kind, but that was a risk I would not take. So after a term these activities came to a natural end. Many were the slabs of toffee, bars of chocolate, lead soldiers of every sort, and packets of Plasticine I had brought in without (I think) being detected. Some goodwill had been earned, and over that early career of amateur crime I have few regrets. A year later Teddy went on to the Upper School as a boarder, and I as a day-boy in the Preparatory saw little of him except in the holidays.

In Scotland, where pagan customs have a tendency to linger on, Hallowe'en was celebrated with warmth and excitement, for that was the evening when ghosties and witches were abroad and at their most dangerous. Mother organised our celebrations on a generous scale, inviting some children from neighbouring houses. In one part of our vegetable garden there was a forest of artichoke plants, through which Helena and I had cut a winding pathway. We made turnip lanterns, and as soon as it was really dark we donned our fierce masks and led parties through this forest swinging our weird lanterns to scare away any spooks and bogles, witches and boggarts that might try to harm us.

Indoors after a grand tea-party we had 'dookin' for apples, when each of us stood on a chair and fork in mouth dropped it to spear one of the apples floating in a pail on the floor. The climax was 'snap-dragon' in the servants' hall, when all the lights were turned out and Father put a match to a great ashet of raisins and nuts soaked in brandy. The blue flames leaped in the darkness and brave hands, miraculously unburnt, picked out the warm lighted fruits and, blowing them out, popped them into our mouths.

When I was eight Mother gave me a new bicycle and taught me to ride it in our road, Hermitage Drive, so that I could join several Merchiston boys who had the freedom of the roads. There was very little other traffic to trouble us: the milkman whose patient horse knew exactly where and when to stop; an occasional delivery van; perhaps the odd cab; certainly our friend the knife-grinder pushing his ancient and ingenious trolley from house to house; and each evening the bicycling lamplighter, leaning in turn against the street-lamps while his long pole with shielded flame was poked up through the base of the lamp to ignite the gas-jet.

The summer term brought cricket, and those long lazy afternoons when, after a usually brief appearance before the stumps, one was free to lie on a grassy bank and drowsily watch the play. Sometimes we were joined by an extraordinary character, name unknown, whom we addressed as 'Ranji' after the famous cricketer. He was a tall man between fifty and sixty, always punctiliously dressed in a frock coat and top hat, however hot the weather. Around his rather dirty neck he wore a loudly-striped tie and a tall stiff collar of gutta-percha, grimy with age. He carried with him an old baggy umbrella and his telescope. This last item, about three feet long, was composed entirely of rolled newspapers held together with glue. It was his custom, in the full afternoon sun, to gaze through it into the blue sky and comment on the various stars and galaxies that he recognised in their appointed orbits. He was, of course, a little touched, and his home was Craighouse Lunatic Asylum. Yet he knew *Wisden's Cricketing Almanack* almost by heart, and could tell you not only the results of any inter-school match in the Edinburgh area over the past ten years, but probably the number of runs scored by any individual player on each occasion.

I blush to recall how rude we were to him, not understanding his condition. We called out cheeky remarks and challenged him to attack us with his umbrella. But, being a man of few words, he never answered back and refused to be provoked; and presently we would sit close beside him, cautiously laying a hand on his shoulder, so that he probably knew we were friendly at heart. He had a soft spot for me, having been a spectator on the only occasion when I ever did the hat-trick. In the 'under-tens' anything could happen; and this time it did. My first ball was a straight one and therefore not surprisingly took a wicket; the second was skied by the new batsman and fell into the hands of long-leg who, after juggling with it for a time, clutched it to his breast; the third was bowled in such a frenzy of excitement that the batsman blindly whirled his bat round his head and fell backwards onto his wicket.

Ranji was a regular supporter of Merchiston's 1st XI; but he probably found better entertainment in the scatter-brained light-hearted cricket of the 'under-tens'.

Another eccentric personality to be seen along the Colinton Road in those days was Theodore Napier, about whom I never knew more than my eyes told me. He was a magnificent bearded figure, wearing a kilt, a fine jacket with silver buttons, and a plaid gathered on one shoulder with a huge cairngorm set in an antique silver mount. Had this costume been in colourful tartan it would have been impressive enough; but his garb was throughout of hodden grey cloth, perfect for concealment among rocks and heather, and worn in the centuries before tartan colours took the fashion; and its very greyness seemed all the more to catch the eye and invest the wearer in mystery. Over this he wore a great studded sword-belt, though memory fails to tell me if he actually carried a sword. His feet were shod in deer skin with laces criss-crossed up his stockings; and the right leg bore a black and jewelled *skian dhu* of triple daggers. From his neck and wrists came a froth of old lace; and to crown all he wore a grey bonnet with a silver brooch and a huge eagle's feather which stood aloft like a shining sword blade. It was as if by some trick of time this swashbuckler from the days of Montrose and Charles I had stepped into the twentieth century, and whenever I spied him striding alone and purposeful along the Colinton Road I would get over to the other side and keep my fingers crossed.

In a Minister's home it was natural that some of the pictures should be of religious subjects. But there was one which seemed to me to push its theme rather too far, especially as it hung in a prominent position in our lovely dining-room. It was an engraving of the Last Judgment by Gustav Doré. The upper part of this ghastly picture portrayed clouds of glory and angels blowing trumpets at the serried ranks of the Eternally Blessed. Below, at the direction of the Avenging Angel, multitudes of agonised and naked humans fell hurtling into a bottomless abyss. This did not make the next world appear a very inviting place for either the bad or the good. I believe Doré was mad. At any rate looking at the picture made me feel quite giddy, and when I found myself hesitating to walk along the tops of high walls I thought it time to take counter-measures. Wearing gym-shoes my brother and I climbed out of a dormer-window and started to explore the Drum-earn roofs. This was quite thrilling, and such was our confidence in the gripping power of our rubber soles that no part of the roof or chimney-stacks remained for long unconquered. We were sure of foot and of balance from racing over the seaweedy rocks at North Berwick, and it never occurred to us that the tiles might give way. Mother saw us but, to our surprise, made no comment. I think she wanted us to be adventurous, and relied on Teddy's judgment if not on mine.

Father too could sometimes behave in a surprising way. That August we moved to the parish of Kirkmichael in the Cromdales, to give the Minister a holiday. There was plenty of trout-fishing, and he had taken me over to Brig-o'-Brown where we caught three good ones. Walking home through the heather I noticed we were being rapidly fol-lowed by a keeper with two large dogs. These were barking and there was an occasional shout from the man, but Father paid no attention. It occurred to me that we might have been wrong in taking three such good fish, and I sug-gested that there was still time to hide them in the heather and pick them up later; but Father did not agree. Before long, because of my short legs, the keeper caught up with us, and challenged us angrily. My guilty conscience made a coward of me, and I could not see how Father could pos-sibly get out of it. But he just drew himself up, glared at the keeper and said slowly and majestically, 'Don't you know who I am?'

The effect was surprising. The keeper lost his nerve, said, 'Sorry, sir', mumbled something about being mistaken;

then, touching his cap, he called off his dogs and turned back the way he had come. Even now I sometimes wonder what would have happened if the keeper had replied, 'Well, who are you?' It is true Father was the son of a dead Lord Advocate, but he never traded on that. Since then I have come to the view that it was not only Father but the keeper who was bluffing; that we had done nothing illegal after all; and that when Father stood up to him, he saw the danger signals flying and made off. But it certainly showed my Father in a new light, and I stored the incident in my memory.

Among other parishes where we went for the August holidays Nethybridge remains sadly in the memory, for on every day of that month we had a downpour. The Manse, a fine stone building with ornamental knobs, stood close to the river; and from its windows we watched the brown foaming Nethy, bank-high, leaping and roaring down to join the Spey. Fishing was impossible, so we spent much of the time doing trick-cycling among the dripping trees until clouds of midges drove us indoors.

Another year saw us at Killin at the foot of Loch Tay, the opposite end from Pontius Pilate's reputed birthplace. That year it was very hot. The taps in the Manse ran dry, and every drop of water had to be carried in buckets from the loch; and by us. Luckily there were no water-closets in the Manse. Instead, there was an old wooden earth-closet at the foot of the garden. After some murmuring we soon found there was much to be said for this old-fashioned device. For one thing the unvarnished wooden seat was always warm. For another there was plenty of natural ventilation and it always smelt clean. A little hole in the door gave a view up the garden path, and the occupant had time to give a discreet cough, or even to burst into song, before anyone could reach the door. Mother just said, 'What's simplest is often best', and we all agreed with her. She had a wonderful way of making light of difficulties. She would have done well at Lucknow.

I realise now how fortunate we were to have a Mother who was self-propelled, who never complained or appeared discouraged at our seeming lack of appreciation. The fact is that she worked on a different level from ours — both higher and deeper. And now it is too late to tell her so.

9
The Indian Year

In 1906 the Church of Scotland asked Father if he would go to India to take the duty at Simla for a year. He consulted Mother, who 'jumped at the idea'. In her memoirs she says, 'It would be too long a story to go into our life in India', so my account will be brief indeed.

Father left by sea in the autumn. Mother arranged for Teddy and me to board at Merchiston, and for Agnes, our trusty and beloved table-maid, to take Helena to the Aunts. In the holidays we were to return to Drumearn where Miss Keith, a charming lady and qualified nurse, would take care of us.

Mother sailed for India in the early spring. From Bombay she went to Simla by train and there joined Father. When his spell of duty ended in October, they embarked on a sight-seeing tour before returning home. They stayed at Lahore with the Lieutenant-Governor of the Punjab, whose wife had befriended Mother on the ship from England.

At the station I was amazed to find a most luxurious equipage awaiting us, no less than the Camel Carriage used by the L.G. himself, a most delightful barouche drawn by four lovely camels on each of which were Indian riders in most attractive white uniforms trimmed with crimson and gold, and gorgeous turbans, and saddles covered with leopard skins. I longed that the family might have seen it.

There they found and photographed the grave of Major Frank Constant, her father.

Thence to Lucknow ('And ever upon the topmost roof our banner of England blew'), Cawnpore, Benares, the burning ghats on the Ganges, Calcutta, Darjeeling and Everest. In a dandy on the shoulders of four strong Tibetans Mother was carried to Kalimpong, and saw in the hospital the bed they had subscribed for, with 'Monzievaird' on the plate at its head. After a fortnight in Burma they came back to Agra, saw the Taj Mahal by moonlight; then on to Rajputana, 'where we stayed at Mhow, my birthplace, and saw my mother's grave. My last lovely memory was the sight of Udaipur with its white palaces on islands in the lake, all salmon pink in the rays of the setting sun, and a range of purple and grey mountains in the distance.'

They were home in time for Christmas.

For children aged thirteen, nine and five the loss of their parents for a year was a new experience that gave rise to some anxious questionings. How long really was a year going to be? And what might not happen to prevent them ever coming home again? Of course we each received a weekly letter or a highly-coloured postcard, but that did little to make up for our loss of personal contact. And we in turn had the wearisome Sunday task of writing to our unseen parents; and found ourselves so barren of ideas that in the end our letters can have done little more than reflect the polite inquiries and good wishes of those who dictated them to us.

Helena, now installed with the Aunts at Tunbridge Wells, at first found life rather different from her Drumearn régime. On Sunday she brought out all her dolls and was quietly playing with them when the Aunts entered and caught her in the very act. How dare she? Didn't she know it was the Lord's Sabbath and that all games were forbidden (even solitaire!) in order that her thoughts could be concentrated on higher things? In vain Helena pleaded with tears, 'But they are not just dollies; they are my family!' It was no good. She was given a text to learn — 'Thou God seest me' — which, whatever it may mean or imply to grown-ups, suggested to Helena a kind of hide-and-seek in reverse, or even the Peep-Bo of baby days. Agnes, with infinite tact, apparently succeeded in humanising the situation, for some time later Mother in India received the following:

Dear Madam,

Miss Helena is quite happy now and not at all home-sick, and she is so good and so very comical. It is most amusing to hear her holding long conversations with some imaginary persons. The other day she dressed up as Mrs Spinks and pretended she was calling on the Aunts, and there she sat for I'm sure half an hour and talked about everything you could think of to Miss Constant. She told her all about her five children, two girls and three boys, but she could not remember all their names, and we asked the name of her husband and she said it was Arthur and then she forgot she had said that and told us it was Matthew and when we reminded her that Arthur was what she had said first, she said 'Oh, yes, but he was an old man and he is dead now and I've married this other one.' She did it awfully well and we were all screaming with laughter and she looked so solemn about it.

How Ted got on in the Castle I couldn't tell as I never saw him in term-time. My own fortunes were varied. The cement play-ground in the Preparatory School was perfect for long slides, and on frosty mornings we were at it even

before school began. Latin, with which I had been on distant terms for a year past, now became a subject more
demanding. It was taught by a new master who had a club
foot, a glass eye, and a good selection of comic songs at
the piano. At first we browsed uninspired over *Kennedy's
Latin Primer*, and I was not the only one who got a licking
as a stimulant. This unpleasant experience consisted of up
to six on the hands with a 'tawse' or thick leather strap
with four tails. Our master hardened the tails by soaking
them in whisky, as I discovered by the smell when I was
sent to his study to fetch the strap. If the tails struck the
tender front of the wrist they could draw blood, but in
that case the victim could complain to the Headmaster,
thus gaining a moral victory; so that didn't often happen.
This was not the only licking I had, and I soon developed
the technique of holding my hand out to one side, and at
the moment of impact moving it a couple of inches towards the striker which I thought slightly lessened the
pain.

One of the boys was much admired and envied because,
through an accident with an air-gun, he had lost all sensa-
tion in the palm of his right hand. His nonchalance under
punishment astonished the masters, and the rest of us
never betrayed his secret. But none of all this really helped
me to make much sense of Dr Kennedy's immortal work.

Then one day our Latin master appointed two form
captains with power to select their own teams. Half an
hour was allowed for studying Latin grammar and play
then began, each side questioning the other. After some
weeks of this most of us knew our grammar well, and by
the end of the term several were scoring 100 per cent
including the Gender Rhymes. I specialised in

> Many Nouns in '-is' we find
> to the Masculine assigned:
> amnis, axis, caulis, collis,
> clunis, crinis, fascis, follis,

fustis, ignis, orbis, ensis,
panis, piscis, postis, mensis,
torris, unguis, and canalis,
vectis, vermis, and natalis,
sanguis, pulvis, cucumis,
lapis, casses, Manes, glis.

For this I held the speed record of 9 seconds flat; and can still do it, just.

Rugger also was taught as a discipline. Our games were refereed by Castle Prefects who were members of the school 1st XV; heroes to us. Attached to the referee's whistle was a plaited leather thong, called a 'twistie', which might cut across the bottom of any forward not pushing his weight in the scrum, or of any of the backs who shirked their tackles. But it was rarely used. Even in the Prep School we played a hard game, not without its ferocious moments, as we tried to impersonate the great Scottish players whom we supported with such fervour in the International matches at Inverleith.

In the Easter holidays Teddy and I visited London at the invitation of Uncle John. He had a wonderful flat in Princes Gate, with a butler, a lift and fresh flowers everywhere; and a private box at the Albert Hall. Several of his family were with him, but they were all older than we were. Everything was very different from Edinburgh: the horse-buses, the cosy hansoms, the tar in the Kensington streets to deaden the wheels when some important person was ill; the muffin man with his bell; the crossing-sweeper to whom Uncle John gave twopence every time he crossed the road.

Uncle John was then M.P. for Brighton and Hove, and had a house down there too. He took us to Eastbourne where we met tall, white-haired Uncle George and prim little Aunt Ellen. And we even had tea with Aunt Lena of whom we had heard so much from Mother. Our Great Aunt was an enormous woman, beautifully dressed in black silk with white frills, for she was in mourning for her husband. She had several double chins, a glass eye, and a toupée which tended to be slightly and ludicrously off balance. From her massive bust there descended a rope of pearls like a waterfall; and every now and then she made a characteristic gesture of the hand as if dusting off any crumbs that might have lodged on that ample shelf. Her conversation was interspersed with warm chuckles, and when it came to the point her laughter was hilarious, causing her to shake all over like a jelly.

Tea with her was an exquisite occasion. A table-cloth of antique lace; Georgian silver tea-pot, kettle with its methylated spirits burner, and cream-jug; china so delicate that I took the cup in both hands; the thinnest of cucumber sandwiches, hot scones, and chocolate cake, for Great-Aunt had a sweet tooth. 'Now, tell me, Huntly. Do you like this jam?' It was made of wild strawberries! 'Yes, Tiptree. I *always* have *Tiptree* jams!' She pronounced the name with such a blend of delicacy and gusto that one couldn't help laughing.

Her late husband was Irish, with a ready sense of humour. When I was older and called on her to say good-bye before going out to France, she told me they had once lived in South Russia, of all places. I did not like to ask why. Certainly not trade; possibly the diplomatic. I asked why they didn't stay there. Her reply was typical. 'My dear, I just didn't care for it, so we came away!' They had no children, though she had a very soft spot for the young. Her husband adored her, and she loved him no less after he had gone. No aunt could ever have been kinder or more understanding.

Teddy and I shared a bedroom at the Dudley Hotel, Hove. We had heard about Captain Webb swimming the Channel, and of course we had to find a way to copy him. In the early morning we stood up on our pillows, dived forward under the bedclothes, swam breathlessly, and on emerging at the foot of the bed claimed we were in

France. Teddy chose to be Captain Webb, so I had to be Burgess, his lesser rival. On the last morning, our competing efforts were so fierce that disaster struck; Captain Webb's bed broke in half and collapsed on the floor! We thought we were really for it, then. However fortune came to our help. On top of our wardrobe we found part of an umbrella without the handle. We remade the bed with extreme care, propped up its middle precariously with the umbrella, and left the hotel before the authorities could challenge us. Confession is good for the soul. Some day I may even call on behalf of Captain Webb and offer to pay for the damage.

The absence of our parents made us children want to draw closer together, and we found that the sharing of secrets helped in this way. Mother must have felt this too, for she took to sending us little messages in looking-glass writing. The scribbles were undecipherable until held before a mirror when at once they became clear to read. Our efforts to imitate this met with so little success, that we concluded that Mother must have done it writing backwards with her left hand, standing on her head. Teddy, however, came up with a language code, through which he and I could talk secretly in front of other people. It consisted simply of interposing 'irig' before each syllable. Thus, Yirigoove girigot mirigai pirigeny — You've got my penny. Simple for us; double-Dutch to the listener. It was perhaps not very polite to other people, but it was comforting to feel we were somehow special.

Teddy and I were closer friends during that year than ever before or since. He once took me to see the first of the moving pictures, at the Synod Hall, Tollcross. It was a rainy day, and the woman who showed us to our seats in the darkness had to guide us with a bull's-eye lantern because there were so many buckets in the aisles catching the rain that dripped from the roof. The place was packed and the tickets were threepence each. We got in for half that price. The film I remember was of a knight in full

armour on a horse, riding to Hell. He rode through an endless series of echoing rocky passages underground, and the
clattering noise of the hooves (off-stage) was realistic
beyond words; and when the picture suddenly turned all
red, presumably from the colour of Hell-fire, it was almost
terrifying.

Teddy also took me to a circus at the Waverley Market,
where Buffalo Bill (Colonel Cody) rode into the ring, a
magnificent figure with flowing white hair, a pointed
beard, and a fine leather coat with a sash across it. His
horse reared up and pranced all round the ring, but the
Colonel never fell off, and made his exit with a flourish of
his hat to great applause.

There was also Fred Lindsay the Whip Wonder, an
Australian stockman who performed marvellously with a
selection of very long whips, each feat ending with a crack
like a pistol shot. At a range of several yards he could snuff
out a candle without upsetting it, flick the ash off the end
of a cigarette held in a girl's mouth, and so flog a girl lying
on the floor that you had to look away, and yet the lash
never touched her. As soon as I got home I made a long
whip from a clothes-line and plaited string, and started in.
It was lucky for Helena that she was still staying with the
Aunts and could not be enlisted as the girl assistant. As it
was I got on well with the candle-snuffing, but abandoned
the whole ploy when the end of the lash caught my right
ear so viciously that for a moment I thought it had been
detached from my head.

Then there was the memorable evening in the Waverley
Market when Teddy and I went to watch Taro Myaki, the
Giant Japanese Wrestler, challenging all comers for a prize
of £5. Two wrestlers were vanquished by the great man,
who was obviously their superior. The next challenge came
from Jim Esson, a huge Glasgow policeman, with a small
crowd of Glasgow supporters. It was a most exciting bout,
and there were cheers when the policeman at last had the
Jap firmly pinned to the floor. But when it was announced

that the Jap had been off the mat, and the £5 would not be paid, loud booing broke out. Jim Esson argued furiously with the referee, and then caught him with a right upper-cut that lifted him clean off his feet. Teddy took my arm and we quickly got out of an exit, leaving behind a free-for-all fight among the audience more exciting than anything we had seen that evening.

10
The Hebrides

Mother and Father returned from India on 23 December 1907, which was also Teddy's fourteenth birthday. The house must have been decorated, and there must have been suitable festivities, but of these I recall nothing. The overwhelming fact, obliterating everything else, was that they were safely home, and life could return to normal after a long year of separation and uncertainty. Yet after that things were never quite the same. Home seemed to have lost something of its security. That strongest of links had been severed once; and for all I knew it might happen again. The fact was that Mother had so dominated our lives that I had been almost lost without her. In those days it seemed that changes were never explained to us in advance, and we were not encouraged to ask questions — a relic probably of the policy that 'children should be seen and not heard'. So we had to learn the hard way that the future should never be taken for granted.

Mother was full of her Indian experiences and able to describe them vividly when asked to address Edinburgh audiences. 'I felt almost like a Medium', she said, 'and the words just poured out of me!' She told her audience how she had given a Purdah party at the Simla Manse; how the women had to be fetched in covered carts so that no man might see them; how one woman to whom Mother had given a supply of 'Mellins' Food' for her ailing little son fell at her feet with gratitude for the boy's recovery; how she took them all by a private way into the Church and sang hymns in which they tried to join; how she had composed a special hymn for them in Hindustani (tune faintly reminiscent of 'Three Blind Mice'); how quick they were to understand the few words of Hindustani that she recalled from childhood now that they were all mothers together. To make her talk more realistic she dressed Helena in a sari with glass bangles and silver anklets whose tiny bells tinkled as she walked; and over all was the white sheet-like garment gathered at head, with only two tiny holes for the eyes, such as Mohammedan women wore in those days if they ever ventured out.

Such was Mother's enthusiasm that she even persuaded me to go with her and Helena to a public party in Morningside Hall, where fancy dress was voluntary. I was to go as a syce, or fore-runner to a carriage. My face and hands were darkened with burnt cork. Over a white cricket shirt I wore a beautifully embroidered Indian waistcoat, with a similar cap on the back of my head. But Mother's proposals for my lower half were beyond all reason, even beyond all decency; black cotton stockings over my knees, and a pair of Helena's white frilly drawers! These were too tight at the knees. Never mind, they could be let out. They had no fly-buttons. Girls didn't need them. Well, I jolly well did. Finally I was made to hold a long garden cane, though whether as a wand of office or a weapon of defence, I didn't know. Feeling, and probably looking, an absolute idiot, I did it just to please Mother.

When we got to the hall and Helena and I appeared in costume things were worse than I feared. Two older boys from the Prep whom I disliked (they came from Glasgow) closed in on me.

'Hey! What the hell are you supposed to be?'

'I'm a syce.'

'A what?'

'A syce. I run through the crowds.'

'Why?'

'I don't really know.'

'Bloody well run then!'

I quickly hid myself in the crowd, hoping that if I kept close enough to people they wouldn't see my drawers. Mother afterwards said I should have won a prize; but I was glad enough to escape without being had up for public indecency.

1908 was the year when the Boy Scout Movement took the headlines. I bought a copy of *Scouting for Boys* and was enthralled. I crept around the garden looking for 'spoor', and examining trees to see which side the prevailing wind came from. The incantation, 'Ingonyama, Ingonyama, invooboo! Yabo, yabo, invooboo!' seemed to give the much-needed confidence that must be such a satisfying feature of any secret society. Mother thoroughly approved, and was prepared to pay for whatever was wanted; so I bought a uniform complete in every detail down to the police-whistle, the knife, the pole and pennant. I chose one with the Beaver sign, as indicating a patrol that would be very busy, and on good terms with Indians.

Well, there I was, fully equipped and eager to start. But where was the rest of the Beaver Patrol? Teddy said he was too old; Helena was disqualified by her sex; Tom Brown, my best local friend, was too busy with his new bike. No one in our corner of Morningside seemed interested. Looking back, I seem to have been very unenterprising; probably because it was usually Mother or Teddy who had taken the lead in our activities. So once again it was Mother who stepped into the breach. Included in the Scouting Manual was a play in full detail called 'Pocahontas, or The Capture of Captain John Smith'. We decided to put it on in Drumearn Theatre, the big upstairs attic.

Our previous plays had been presented with small card-board figures on a stage whose proscenium was about eighteen inches by a foot. The figures, scenery and words printed on one large paper sheet cost threepence. We mounted them on cardboard, making our own footlights and curtain. The 'effects', including tray-thunder, horse-hoofs, icing-sugar snow and gradual sunsets, brought an enthusiastic response from the audience. Sometimes we took a silver collection, mostly threepenny bits, but very welcome.

Now for the first time we were putting on a real live play; with Helena starring as Pocahontas, the Indian Princess, and myself as Captain John Smith exploring the Virginia jungle in 1607. Producer, Hon. Mrs Arthur Gordon. The Virginia jungle was constructed and painted by the family and staff. The action was to extend over a distance of several hundred yards, and it took all Mother's ingenuity to compress it into a stage four yards wide.

When the action begins, Captain Smith is doing all the talking, and while arrows (with rubber suction heads) whizz past, he discharges his gun to a running commentary: 'How now? They run, the dogs! Ha, another bites the dust! Ha! Ha! Well done, thou trusty Bess' (an ironical comment, as the roll of caps had just jammed and there-after Bess only uttered a series of faint clicks). 'Ha! Good, another falls; Gadzooks, have at them again! Aid me, St George, and let me show what stuff an Englishman is made of!' Whereupon Indians overpower the Captain and lash him to a tree in the centre of the stage.

There follows some rather unproductive conversation, John Smith saying what a decent fight they'd had, and how the Indians really deserved to win. Meanwhile noises are heard off-stage as some white devils are seen to be approaching to rescue the Captain. But Princess Pocahontas, who has been giving the Captain a good look-over, rushes to his rescue and cuts his bonds with her dagger. He politely shakes hands with her. Unfortunately the Princess's enthusiasm has also dislodged the tree from the floor, and our hero's beard from his face; so that John Smith, so far from straining away from the tree, is now doing his best to support it vertically behind his back with one hand, while the other holds Trusty Bess and is also busy keeping his beard in place. At this point Mother saved the situation by drawing the curtain.

The last scene or dénouement went more smoothly. The Indian Chief, suddenly breaking into faultless Elizabethan English, decides to surrender. 'Fair sir, we yield; and on our oath we swear allegiance to your king for aye and ever, weal or woe.' All then raise their hands in the Scout signal. John Smith suddenly produces the banner of St George from beneath his coat, and hooking it on to a Scout's staff waves it aloft. 'Behold the flag of St George and Merry England!' Warriors salute and sing the Ingonyama Chorus; while the Band (Mother) plays 'Rule Britannia', followed by the National Anthem. Ah, great days, great days!

During the summer Mother organised a successful sale of work, at which she persuaded a large number of benevolent ladies to crowd our lawns 'in aid of the heathen'. It was also a good opportunity for them to display the latest fashions in friendly (well, fairly friendly) rivalry. Their gorgeous hats, some carrying at least two tiers of full-blown cabbage roses, put our garden flowers in the shade. Their white kid gloves, long flouncing dresses, veils and feather-boas made an impressive sight as they crowded round the garden-tables loaded with such knick-knacks and fripperies as might induce them to spend freely in such a good cause.

141

We children all had a part to play. Helena was dressed once more in her Zenana costume, and limped about the sharp gravel paths in bare feet and glass bangles. Hidden in a summer-house, I maintained a steady output of ice-cream from a revolving drum containing chopped ginger and custard in the central compartment and crushed ice sprinkled with salt in the outer jacket. This machine had to be rotated by hand, a tiresome task only made worthwhile by the need for frequent sampling. Teddy plied to and from the stalls with loose change, and ran messages for Mother when she and Father were preoccupied with the guests. Towards the end of the sale we three retired to our platforms in the branches of a large chestnut tree and there sat in silence, eating ices and exchanging, through an elaborate system of strings and pulleys, written comments on the guests below which were not for their ears.

In the summer holidays of that year Mother took Helena to Eastbourne, while Father took Teddy and me on a fishing expedition to the Outer Hebrides. It was an unforgettable trip. We sailed from Oban in MacBrayne's *Plover*, bound for Barra. She was an old small steamer, and when after calling at Tobermory she emerged from the Sound of Mull and set out across the Minch in the teeth of a westerly gale, she gave us a terrible ride. Off Ardnamurchan Point huge waves were leaping up and down, and a little further on Teddy and I no longer noticed what they were doing; we were too busy over the rail. Father, his deer-stalker tied securely under his chin, his feet braced against a raft, spread out his Inverness cape as a hen spreads her wings, and we two chicks snuggled underneath and passed into a coma.

After an hour of slow progress, one of the *Plover*'s two engines broke down. With great difficulty the Captain succeeded in rigging a lug-sail. With her speed much reduced the ship's antics increased, and we began to think we would never get to land. The five-hour journey took over twelve hours, and the Isle of Barra itself went on heaving long after we had staggered ashore.

We spent next day recovering in the hotel. Then Father asked if there was any trout-fishing to be had. The manager at first had nothing to suggest; but on being pressed he admitted there was a wee loch, maybe a mile and a bit up the road, but so small that no one bothered to fish it. At this Father sighed and said how disappointing that was; and that as the weather had turned fine and sunny we had better just go for a walk. Teddy and I had already observed that there wasn't much Father didn't know about the art of finding out where to fish and keeping that knowledge to oneself. So without comment we followed him dejectedly out of the hall, and up to our bedrooms. 'A wee loch that no one has bothered to fish; we'll try our luck,' said Father.

We tied our three rods into one bundle to avoid attention; Teddy carried a school satchel; and we left by the side door. As we walked Father explained that the local folk found it easier to get their fish out of the sea, and probably didn't bother with fresh-water fishing; so for all they knew there might be a chance for us.

We found the little loch gleaming like a jewel in the bright sunshine; but there was such a thick growth of weed that it seemed impossible to get a fly on to the open water, and of course there was no boat. But Father was undeterred. I began to wonder whether his religious faith had not spilled over and affected his fishing. He led us round the shore and on the far side we found a gap in the weed, with a shallow sandy bottom showing through. He took off his stockings, rolled up his breeks and, wading out, succeeded in casting his flies along the edge of a great bank of water-lilies. Before long he was into a fish. It took a good quarter of an hour to play it out, and then he brought ashore an enormous trout of lovely colouring. The whole thing seemed like a miracle.

Ted was next. The miracle was repeated; this time 1½ lbs

to Father's three-pounder. At last it was my turn, and to keep my shirt dry I went in wearing only a pair of rolled-up shorts. The water was over my waist before casting was possible. Soon I too had my reward, a nice quarter-pounder. We were fully content with one fish each, because it had been a thrill to overcome these difficulties, and to be greedy would have spoilt it. Father and Ted went into the village and gave away their catch without saying where it had come from. And when I entered the hotel with my little fish and asked to have it for my supper the manager humoured me, smiling a superior smile, as much as to say 'I told you so.' And thus the wee loch was allowed to keep its secret.

Next day we took the steamer for the short but lively run to Loch Boisdale in South Uist. South Uist was a world of its own. No trains, no trees, and the scenery bleak; though it has two fine mountain-peaks. August was not a good fishing month that year, and after a week of disappointing weather we hired a horse-drawn 'brake' and drove northwards to Benbecula. To reach this island we had to cross half a mile of sea. But not by boat. The road sloped down to the shore and disappeared under the water and we followed the road. The horses trusted the driver, and the driver navigated the brake by guiding it from one marked rock to another, for the under-sea road was anything but straight. The sea was fairly calm, but at times the floor-boards were awash and we had to lift up our feet. The driver agreed that if he lost his way we might founder in the soft sand; which was why he took care not to lose his way. To Teddy and me it was all very exciting, but Father remained serenely calm. It would be only slightly blasphemous to suggest that if we had gone down he might conceivably have been able to step out and walk ashore. But Teddy and I, weighed down with our sins, could not hope to achieve that. Presently, however, the roadway reappeared as the water shallowed, and we stepped out on dry land.

We stayed a week in the Creagorry Inn. Our ghillie was Archie MacDougal, a dark man of middle age with a deep voice whose slow English carried the enchanting music of his native Gaelic. He taught Teddy and me the art of flounder-spearing, which we found more exciting though less skilled than trout-fishing. The spear was made by lashing a big nail on to the end of a long stick. Armed with this you go wading at low tide in the shallow sandy pools, keeping on the alert for quicksands.

It is very difficult to spot a flounder when it lies motionless on the sandy bottom. You grope forward with your foot until you disturb one. It swims away for a few yards, there is a flurry of sand, and it has vanished. Stealthily you approach the spot. The fish must be almost under your nose, but where? If the light is right and the water calm you may think you see the target, a flattened ripple in the sand. You allow something for the bending effect of the water and plunge in your spear. This is the great moment. If you are lucky you wave the flounder aloft in triumph. More often you have only speared sand. Teddy had plenty of opportunity for derisive laughter. Never mind. Next time lucky.

The best day of all was when Archie took me out in his boat on the mill-pool fishing for sea-trout. He let me take an oar, and then chose a bright fly and showed me how to cast better. He was full of stories of life in the Hebrides, the fearful storms, the rescue of sailors from wrecked ships. As he spoke, he produced from his pocket something like a stick of liquorice, which he cut up with a knife in the palm of his hand and stuffed into an old briar pipe fitted with a perforated metal lid.

While I was watching this ritual there came an almighty tug, and I was on. The fish went mad. I jumped to my feet and might have gone overboard if Archie had not firmly held me down. Eventually Archie netted and killed it. Walking on air, I carried back to the hotel my first one-pounder and displayed it on the hall table. In the fishing book I recorded the catch, adding in the remarks column the casual note 'wind gusty', as others before me had sometimes done. But this time it really meant 'Glory Hallelujah!'

On Sunday Father took the church service. Archie was stationed in the pew behind us with a stick, in case Teddy and I created a disturbance. We were in our kilts, and during the sermon something started tickling the back of my knee. I naturally turned on my brother, a movement which caused the crawling wasp to drive in its sting — ouch! Archie gripped his stick and uttered a 'Wheesht!' which echoed round the little church and drew a reproving glance from the pulpit. The wasp finished up on the floor under my heel, and I spent the rest of the service praying that Father would finish quickly and let me get back to the hotel for the blue-bag.

At the end of the week we said goodbye to Archie, and set out for Loch Maddy in another horse-drawn vehicle called simply 'a machine'. This time we had to ford a much wider stretch of water which could only be risked at low tide with a fairly calm sea. The wind was rising but the driver said the risk was worth taking so long as we were not caught by the incoming tide. So once more we found ourselves following an invisible road through a wide expanse of sea. The fresh wind was building up the ripples into waves during our half-hour crossing, but at last we pulled out thankfully onto dry land, and set off across the moor.

In the afternoon our steamer left North Uist for Dunvegan in Skye, but now the gale was behind us. Father had dosed me heavily with bromides, and this time I was in a dream-like state hanging on to the rail, and riding the seas with reckless delight as the seething waves caught up, and passed, and fell away from the ship's sides.

Of our landing at Dunvegan I was hardly aware. The crisp grinding of iron-shod wheels woke me from time to time as our machine drove through the night across Skye to Portree — a lovely night of moonlight and stars and scudding clouds, seen from under Father's Inverness cape. And so to bed at the inn. Next morning, breakfast in the room where Bonnie Prince Charlie parted from Flora Macdonald. Then a few hours on another steamer in sheltered waters south to Mallaig, and a train journey, and at last my bed at Drumearn.

While we were away Mother had taken Helena on a round of visits among her relatives in the south. Leaving her with the Aunts, Mother, in company with Cousin Charlotte, sampled some of the best London plays, for she loved good acting of any sort, even when a touring company came to Edinburgh. Here are some of her abiding impressions of the actors at that time.

There was Lewis Waller in *Bardelys, the Magnificent*, a shimmering figure in chain mail with flashing eyes (belladonna, it was said), quite ravishing! Benson as MacBeth, whose drawling voice and haunted look made you shiver. Martin Harvey, in *The Only Way* going to his death so nobly. And that romantic pair Fred Terry and Julia Neilson in *Henry of Navarre* and *The Scarlet Pimpernel*. They were particular favourites with Edinburgh audiences, for in his little speech of thanks at the end Fred would always refer to Julia as 'my dear companion', which was taken to mean they were not really married, though of course they lived together, and set most of the respectable Edinburgh audience nudging each other almost as if in envy.

Then on a lighter note there was the incomparable and delicious Marie Tempest; Seymour Hicks (the rascal!) and lovely Ellaline Terriss; and of course gallant and debonair Cyril Maude in *The Flag-Lieutenant*. *Charley's Aunt* was admittedly funny, but farces were reckoned to be second-rate and too obvious. One heard that *The Importance of Being Ernest* was clever, though a trifle risqué; but of course Oscar Wilde was a name one simply did not mention.

Father would no doubt have enjoyed some of these, and as a worshipper of Sir Walter Scott he longed to see any of the Waverley novels that were offered as plays; but it would have been wrong for a Minister to be seen in the audience. With *Peter Pan* it was different. The whole family went to that, father in an ordinary collar and tie; he and Mother found it very moving, while we children found it very exciting, mainly because on the stage the children could fly, as we had sometimes dreamed we might. And when news came that a Frenchman, Blériot, had flown a machine across the Channel, even though he lost his way, flopped down at Dover Castle and was arrested by a policeman, we all became flying enthusiasts overnight.

Of course we had heard that the Wright Brothers had briefly lifted themselves off the ground in America some years before; but that seemed just a trick, and you had only to see a picture of the machine to know it couldn't really fly. Blériot's monoplane, however, had a distinctly bird-like look, and with its crossing of the Channel flying became a reality. We started to make toy gliders out of cardboard, bamboo, and Seccotine, and thus discovered for ourselves some of the principles of glider flight. Mother brought added enthusiasm to the members of the Drumearn Flying Club by discovering in a Princes Street toyshop a kind of aeroplane shaped like a triangular kite, fitted with a propeller driven by a wound-up elastic cord. She bought two to encourage rivalry, and the race was on! Here at last was something in which I had a chance to beat Teddy, and soon aeroplanes were not only flying all over our garden but being retrieved from our neighbours' as well. Teddy impersonated Claude Graham-White, the leading British pioneer, while I assumed in turn the roles of Blériot, Paulhan, Moore-Brabazon and even Wilbur Wright himself in repeated unsuccessful efforts to avoid defeat by my taller elder brother.

In the holidays Teddy and I competed at golf on the

nine-hole miniature golf-course which we had laid out in the back garden; also on the full eighteen-hole course on the Braid Hills. But on neither of those could I give him a close game without receiving a handicap, which to me spoilt the spirit of the thing. Surely the fun is in the playing of the game, more than merely deciding who is the winner. Handicaps can lead to bitter disputes, and when the persistent winner cannot resist crowing over the persistent loser, even brothers can fall out, as Cain did with Abel. For me the explosion point was coming near; so I determined to find some way of beating Ted at his own game, and without a handicap. Ten days before our next holiday athletic meeting I quietly went into training. Then at Sunday lunch when the whole family was present, I opened my plan.

'I don't see why our Sports events must always be decided by Teddy. He always wins everything.'

'That's your fault, isn't it? But if you've got any suggestions, let's hear them. I'll bet I can beat you anyway.'

'Right. How about a Marathon? Fifty times round the house. Run you for sixpence.'

'Don't be absurd! You couldn't run fifty times round the house.'

'I could try. Of course, if it's too far for you, then forty times. I challenge you. Go on, Mum, make him! He's no sport.'

'Well, you've asked for it,' said Mother to me. 'Go on, Teddy, show him.'

'All right then,' said Teddy. 'I think it's silly, but I'll do it. See you have your sixpence ready.'

On the afternoon of the Sports we had a good turn-out of school friends. Mother had arranged the presents, mostly packets of sweets beautifully tied up in coloured ribbon; some books, some golf balls, and some silver coins twisted up in paper; all set out on a table. She had also ordered a slap-up tea.

The handicap races began, the jumping, the shot-put,

even tossing a small caber. As usual Teddy had a big share of the wins. Then came the Marathon, forty times round the house, one at a time against the clock. There were only three entries and we drew lots for the starting order. Luck was with me; first Teddy, then me, then the other entry. The distance was just on four miles, with a hundred and sixty sharp turns.

Ted set off, started by Mother, while all the rest of us settled down on the grass to watch. He went three times round at a cracking pace, and then slowed down realising he couldn't keep it up. Then some of his friends started teasing him, which didn't go down at all well. He did fifteen rounds, and then pulled up, saying he'd done enough. There was a general protest. Rules were rules.

'Well,' said Teddy, 'I'll make it twenty,' and went off again.

'Yes,' said Mother, 'that will be quite enough, I'm sure; and tea will be ready by then.'

After the twentieth circuit he stopped and picked up his coat. I was ready to start.

'Tea-time,' Mother announced. 'Come on all of you.'

'Forty was what you agreed, Teddy,' I called, and was off round the corner.

Normally I am not much of a runner, but the thought of beating my brother brought a new strength surging inside me and increased my speed. After a while some of the others came out from tea, and called to Ted that I was faster than him. I heard Ted say, 'He'll give up presently.' That was enough. I had got a second wind by now, and running had become almost a pleasure.

When the twentieth round was done, Mother tried to stop me. I just said, 'Out of the way, Mum,' and went on. Forty times or bust, I thought, counting off each circuit as it was done. Meanwhile Mother and Ted started some of the other events. At last came the fortieth round, and they gathered at the winning post, raising a cheer. I swerved past and went grimly on. They probably didn't know what was driving me; but Ted and Mother may have guessed.

Tired, gasping, but happy, I completed the fiftieth round. Mother's protests were ignored. The third competitor declined to run at all. I held out my hand to Ted, and got my sixpence. 'Why fifty?' was all he said. 'Just because you said I couldn't do it,' was my reply. Mother and he must have done some thinking, for the teasing was noticeably less after that.

With Ted's sixpence and a shilling of my pocket money saved over the previous three weeks, I bought a tin of dark tobacco, and sent it as a present to Archie MacDougal in far-away Benbecula. His laboriously written letter of reply I still keep in my ditty-box.

For games of fun I now turned to Father, who somehow was always able to find the time for golf. He was a member of the Mortonhall Club beyond the Braid Hills. There he kept his clubs carefully locked up in a locker with his name on it; though it was difficult to believe that clubs of such ancient design would have tempted anyone seeking to improve his game. Of his five clubs only two had metal heads, the mashie and the niblick. The driver, the baffy and the putter each had a wooden banana-shaped head with a massive ingot of lead melted in along the back. In the case of the putter this did not matter much; but where a long shot was required from the other two, the player was almost compelled to hit mainly with his right hand. (I write as one who has at last seen the light, though now the vision has come too late.) Father's cricket-bat style had blended with his golf swing to produce an inevitable slice. He had not sought anyone's advice about his malady, and I was in no position to offer him any. He tried to cure his fault by drawing back his left foot, which made it worse. So he allowed for it by aiming away to the left and hoping the ball would veer round and end up on the line to the hole. Sometimes it did; but sometimes, so cussed a game is golf, his shot would go where he was aiming it, and land deep in the left-hand rough or sometimes even on the fairway of an adjoining hole. My own play was also erratic, in different ways. So Father usually won the round, and I was content occasionally to win a hole. But our play provided much mutual entertainment, in spite of the time we spent looking for lost balls. Best of all was the lesson he gave me in self-control, for in spite of giving himself every kind of provocation, Father never swore.

There was another game that Father enjoyed: curling. When we left Monzievaird the congregation had presented him with a pair of curling-stones, of the very best grey granite from Ailsa Craig. These, together with a short broom, a pair of galoshes and a black cap with ear-flaps, he kept in a corner of his study, waiting for the frost. And when the day came he would telephone for a cab and drive along Hermitage Drive to Green Bank, where someone would already have flooded the rink. Of the dozen old men there assembled, Father was about the youngest and one of the least good. More than once when he seemed to launch his stone a little clumsily it did not even reach the cross-line; whereupon, amid delighted cries of, 'Ye're a hog, ye're a hog, ye're a hog!' his stone was pushed aside by his opponents' brooms. But I never stayed long as a spectator. To do that you needed to be muffled up to the eyes, with a bottle of something in your pocket, and a brazier to stand over.

Father never missed a chance of passing on a bit of local history. Once when leaving the rink he walked me up the Old Braid Road towards the city, and just where the road begins to go downhill again he showed me a square of granite setts in the middle of the road. 'That was the base of the gallows,' he said, 'where two men were hanged for stealing.' I looked at the spot with a shiver, and fancied I saw them there, wry-necked and dangling — perhaps the desperate fathers of two starving families — and the chains creaking as the bitter wind swung them to and fro.

But let us be fair to the Lord Justice Clerk of the day. According to the *Edinburgh Courant* of 22 December 1814, it was by no means the first time that these two men had committed highway robbery. This time 'they attacked David Loch, the carrier from Biggar, and nearly killed him. They robbed him of four one pound notes, twenty shillings in silver, a two-penny loaf of bread, and a spleuchan or leather tobacco-pouch.' Their execution was watched by a great crowd who had walked in the snow three miles from Edinburgh High Street. That was the last execution in Scotland for highway robbery.

For things to be historically interesting they had to be gruesome. This principle Father either absorbed from his own Victorian environment or devised afresh for my benefit. Thus he took me to Tanner's Close and showed me the very doorway through which Burke and Hare ('the Resurrection Men') had enticed their victims, to suffocate them and sell their bodies to the Dissecting Rooms. Although it looked quite an ordinary doorway, if rather shoddy, I made a mental note never to go near it again, lest by some trick of time I too should make a premature appearance on the slab.

On another occasion when we visited Holyrood Palace, my chief recollection is of seeing on a staircase-landing the dark bloodstains of David Rizzio, the guitar-playing favourite of Mary, Queen of Scots. His vocal unpopularity with the Scottish nobles was apparent from the fifty-six stab-wounds which according to Father were found on his corpse. Those eloquent stains on the floor-boards have now been replaced by a dreary brass plate. Father would be horrified if he knew.

I once went by train with him to St Andrew's, not (as I would have preferred) to walk round that inspired golf-course, but to visit the castle where John Knox was captured by the besieging French and consigned to the galleys. Father had a great respect for John Knox in spite of his rudeness to the Queen. He also showed me the

Bottle Dungeon, a dark pit hewn out of the solid rock, into which I gazed down uneasily. In the good old days, as the name implies, it had neither fresh air, light, water, drainage, nor exit; and most of those thrown in were simply left to rot. Now, since the Ministry of Works have taken it over, conditions are much improved.

Within the circle of our family Father sometimes allowed himself a freedom of criticism which would have been unseemly elsewhere. It was thus his custom to refer to Lord Gordon's family physician as 'that old scoundrel George Keith'. When Father was fourteen Dr Keith, who was said to be partial to huge meals of oysters and salmon, considered him undernourished, and directed that for three weeks he must drink a pint of porter daily. Father loathed the stuff, and before long developed jaundice which he attributed directly to the doctor's treatment. For all that, Father was fair-minded enough to pass on to me one fact in favour of the 'O.S.' He was one of the three doctors who first tried on themselves the effect of chloroform as an anaesthetic. In fact Father took me to Queen Street, and pointing to a window in No. 52, the house of Sir James Simpson, announced, 'That was the dining-room where they did it.'

It appears that Sir James, who was interested in volatile liquids, had an untried bottle of chloroform. He poured some into three tumblers and the doctors sat round the table, and started to inhale deeply. A moment later his wife entered and found all three unconscious on the floor. Simpson was the first to come round, proclaiming, 'This is better than ether.' Dr Keith next emerged, kicking convulsively. As soon as all three were recovered, they persuaded Simpson's niece to inhale the vapour. Fired with enthusiasm, she too passed quickly out, exclaiming that she was joining the angels. Thus casually, indeed comically, the way was opened to the immeasurable benefits of surgery, when painless and unhurried.

11
County Wicklow

1910 was the last year in which we were able to lead carefree lives without thought of the future. Before very long the party would have to break up, and it was as well that we did not think about it. Of course in a sense we were already drifting apart, for Ted (16) was a boarder at Merchiston Castle, I (12) was a day-boy at the Preparatory, and Helena (8) was already launched as a boarder in the Girls' School at North Berwick. But at least we were still together in the holidays.

Edinburgh in that year was the centre for the meeting of the World Missionary Conference. Mother's immense energy had been enlisted for work on the Committee for Hospitality responsible for arranging accommodation for hundreds of delegates from all over the world. 'Quite wonderful were those crowded meetings,' she wrote, 'but it was an eye-opener to see how few of the Anglicans were present, compared with the world-wide representation of

155

the Free Churches. The only section of the Church Catholic not represented at all was that belonging to Rome.' Mother always was outspoken, especially in matters on which she felt deeply.

She hardly missed one of the endless series of Committee meetings concerned with this world-wide event, and when the Conference was on she had our house full of delegates. 'When all was over, the strain I had been through proved rather too much, and I fell in a faint on the landing one morning. However a day in bed soon put me on my feet again.'

On 6 May King Edward VII died. We all saw his funeral procession on the cinematograph. One could not fail to note the arrogance of the German Kaiser, as he rode in procession only half a horse's length behind our new King, George V. His white horse, white-plumed hat, white buckskin breeches, and the blaze of stars and medals covering his breast outshone the darker mourning uniform of our own King. But what came across above all was the Kaiser's arrogant demeanour, his upturned moustaches, and the air of contempt which he displayed towards the crowd. There was no mistaking it, out of place as it was on such a sad occasion. The only Germans I had seen before were the German brass bands who picked up a living playing their mournful melodies in the back streets of Edinburgh. Most of them were fat bespectacled men with heavy blond moustaches and ill-fitting uniforms, with no apparent arrogance in their make-up.

But there was one German of whom I had a closer view, Herr Wurtemann, our music master at Merchiston. He was a bull of a man with a thick neck and no sense of humour. His red and purple face was disfigured with duelling scars, of which he was said to be intensely proud. His bulging blood-shot eyes suggested an apoplectic temper which made us wary of him, particularly when he faced thirty or forty of us gathered in the big school-room for singing.

It was some weeks before the School Concert that he announced, 'I haf a sonk for you today. Here iss paper, and now you write down de vords, hein?'

' "Fot are de pewgles plowing for," set Files-on-Parade'; and Herr Wurtemann slowly dictated the 'sonk' he had chosen. It was not until weeks later that we discovered it was Rudyard Kipling's morbid verse 'Danny Deever'.

For they're hangin' Danny Deever, you can hear the Dead March play,
The regiment's in 'ollow Square — they're hanging him today;
They've taken of his buttons off an' cut his stripes away,
An' they're hangin' Danny Deever in the mornin'.

Someone began to ask a question, but 'Wurtebug' rapped out a command: 'Silence, all of you! Now I vill read it again.' He did so, slowly and with emphasis. 'Now, haf you a question?'

'Yessir,' shouted a dozen voices together.

'Why were they hanging Danny Deever?'

'What's 'ollow Square? How can a square be hollow?'

'You can't say "taken of his buttons off", it isn't English!'

'What did they cut his stripes away with?'

'It's a horrible song, Sir.'

'Why did they bring files on parade, Sir?'

It took Wurtebug a long time to answer these questions, and it took us even longer to disentangle his Germanic English from Kipling's Cockney-Army technicalities. Eventually with Teutonic thoroughness he succeeded in producing at the School Concert a most uninspired rendering of Kipling's unpleasant poem, which no one but Wurtebug would even have thought of as a suitable 'sonk' for schoolboys.

Soon afterwards I heard that this horrible Teuton had actually inflicted a caning on my elder brother. Whether it was deserved or not, I was outraged, and would almost have preferred that he should have beaten me instead. Out of regard for Ted's feelings, I asked no questions; but from then on I had a grudge against Germans.

It was seven years before I saw any more of them at close quarters, and then it was the morning of 31 July 1917, the opening day of the Battle of Ypres/Passchendaele. Near Hell-Fire Corner I met a contingent of German prisoners, sullen and dejected, making their way weaponless and unescorted towards our battery position. Revolver in hand I waved them on towards the Menin Gate. Their leader bowed low and thanked me profusely. Little could they know that their obsequious manner and uplifted hands made some amends for Wurtebug's ruthlessness seven years before.

During the World Missionary Conference Mother and Father renewed their acquaintance with an Irish Baptist missionary, whom they had first met in Delhi, and at his suggestion decided that this year we should break fresh ground by spending our summer holidays in County Wicklow. Mother leased a farm-house near Lough Dan, or to be exact took over the front part of the house, while the regular occupants compressed themselves for a month into the back quarters. A small grassy field in front of the house sloped down to a stream which ran through several deep pools and across a sandy beach into the loch. There were plenty of small trout to be had and, geographically at least, it was a lovely spot for a holiday.

We went by ship to Dublin and by train to Bray, where the Irish missionary and his two sons met us with a large store of flat Irish loaves and a quarter of a sheep. From there we set off for Lough Dan in a Victoria, with a slower cart following containing our luggage, several weeks' supply of food, and the family bath. This last article resembled a large arm-chair without legs and was tastefully painted in light brown to make it look like wood; though anyone who tried to lift it would quickly realise it was of iron. This bath had always been an essential feature of our holiday luggage, for it was able to contain many things of awkward shape, the family sewing machine and a variety of last-minute afterthoughts. We could even bathe in it. It was closed with a large metal lid and secured with ropes, and owing to its weight and awkward shape at least two porters were required to load it on to a train.

On arrival at the farm we found the owner, his wife and children lined up in diminishing order of size to welcome us. Father was distressed to find that, as he greeted each of them, they made a deep obeisance and crossed themselves, saying, 'Your riverince!' In this form of greeting he saw the acknowledgment that a priest had power over them, an idea repugnant to free men, and especially to a Minister of the Church of Scotland.

We all explored the front of the house. On viewing the kitchen Mother was only just able to persuade Annie, our cook, not to return to Scotland forthwith. 'A broken oven surmounted by a swinging kettle and cauldron, a work-table supported at one end on a large stone. Inhabited feather-beds, blankets that have never seen the sun, mat-tresses fit only for a Guy Fawkes pyre — all added to the interest of our Irish sojourn.' This description is taken from our weekly family journal, produced by Ted under the title of the *Lough Dan Chronicle*. At that time Aviation Meetings were big news, and all three of us were soon busy making our own versions of what a glider should be. The sitting-room was littered with thin cardboard, sticky tape, linen and pots of varnish from which we produced gliders launched by hand. The *Chronicle* reporter described our local Meeting in these terms:

On Thursday Lough Dan was the scene of a brilliant spectacle; the gorgeous colour of ladies' dresses; and tents and marquees; aeroplanes flitting across the sky. All the well-known aviators were present, Messrs Grahame-White, Latham, Paulhan, Cody and many others including the Wright brothers, Orville and Wilbur. The Competition results were as follows:

Distance

1st Grahame-White	Distance 12 yards
2nd Wilbur Wright	Distance 10 yards
3rd Drexel	Distance 8 yards.

Altitude

1st Cody	Height 10 ft.
2nd Grahame-White	Height 9 ft. 6 inches
3rd Paulhan	Height 8 ft.

Cross-Country

A long cross-country course, during which the competitors were required to cross a stretch of water of 3 yards breadth was next flown. Total Distance 36 yards.

Mr Santos Dumont took 3 stops, as best effort.

Mr Paulhan	"	3	" ,	" "
Mr Drexel	"	4	" ,	" "
Mr Wright	"	3	" ,	" "
Mr Grahame-White	"	2	" ,	" "

Mr Grahame-White [impersonated by Ted] started last, well aware that he faced the almost impossible task of completing the course with only two stops. But this he achieved. His flying was magnificent. The aviator showed great skill in the manipulation of his machine, and he had a resounding reception at the finish. The cup for the winner of most events was won by Mr Grahame-White. At the end of the meeting, Mr Grahame-White and Mr Paulhan gave an exhibition of flying. The Wright machine was unfortunately damaged by colliding with a tree during its last flight.

(Some twenty years later Ted, by then a doctor with a flourishing London practice, was interviewing patients in his consulting-room in Upper Harley Street. He could hardly believe his ears when his last patient of the morning was announced as 'Mr Claude Grahame-White'. But he maintained a professional calm until the consultation was over. When he told of the outstanding achievements at Lough Dan by Britain's leading flier, there was a good laugh on both sides. Ted continued as Grahame-White's doctor whenever he came to London.)

Before we left Ireland there were two incidents worth recalling. The first concerned the farming family who occupied the back regions of the house, which was out of bounds to us. I must have heard of their old father's death, for I cannot otherwise explain why, choosing a moment when our family were out, I ventured stealthily through the communicating passage and quietly opening the door peered into the big back-room. There was silence and darkness except for six candles arranged in a double row down a long table. On the table were a number of bottles and the preparations for a meal. Looking past the glitter of the candles, I could see at the far end of the table someone seated in a chair. It was an old man with a wizened face; he was dressed in black as for a funeral, and wore an old top-hat tilted drunkenly to one side. 'Sorry, sir,' I said, but he ignored my apology. Then I realised that his staring eyes saw nothing. The guest of honour was a corpse. It gave me the creeps, and I hurriedly withdrew. They told me afterwards that it was an old Irish custom — a 'wake'.

The other incident was for us a real-life tragedy, recorded in the *Lough Dan Chronicle* on pages bordered in deep black.

Great regret will be felt in the Lough Dan district when it is known that Submarine A.1. has been lost with all hands. It was her first trip on the loch and only a few privileged people were present. She had been acquired from the Rossleigh Company last Christmas by Mr Edward Gordon, and had passed her preliminary trials in a big pool in the burn. Her owner then decided to try her on the loch before the official launching took place. Accordingly she was hurried to the water-side, her engines started smoothly and, heading across the cove for the nearby Dublin Point, she began her eventful journey. Diving slightly, she returned to the surface only to be driven off course by a heavy wave. In an instant she was heading out into the loch, and diving again in deep water she disappeared from sight. Two boats at once put out in pursuit, but to no avail. Twice the boats crossed and recrossed

the loch, but when darkness descended they had to return without sighting the submarine. It is understood that the lower end of
the loch will be searched tomorrow, but there is little hope that
she will have drifted unless she has surfaced somewhere.

Extra Late News

This morning a search party examined the whole lower end of the
loch. No trace however was found of the ill-fated vessel. The
cause of the disaster remains a mystery, and with great regret the
owners consider that all hope of survival must now be abandoned.
The Hon. Mrs Arthur Gordon who was to have carried out the
official launching of the vessel has sent messages of sympathy to
the next of kin of the missing crew.

(The vessel had cost £1 15s. 10d., and was not insured.)

The Annual General Assembly of the Church of Scotland
that year promised to be a specially lively affair following
on the World Missionary Conference, and invitations were
sent to the remoter parishes to ensure the fullest possible
attendance of ministers. We had the good fortune to be
host to the Rev. Daniel O'Rork of Muckle Yell in the Shet-
lands, who after tossing at sea for nearly forty hours
arrived at Leith bringing his sister with him. We learned
from a guide-book that Muckle Yell is the northernmost
parish in Scotland; that much of it consists of 'sombre
treeless wastes' and islands inhabited only by seals. Mr
O'Rork and his sister were a silent couple, both with
carroty hair and faces reddened, presumably, by the salt
wind. They were obviously overawed by Edinburgh's
bustle and the contrast between what they saw and what
they were used to.

As we sat at lunch, conversation with our tongue-tied
guests became more and more a matter of questions and
monosyllabic answers. Eventually there was a long silence,
broken only by the Rev. Daniel O'Rork's unusual mannerism
of sucking his soup through his moustache. Feeling that
one more attempt should be made to get the conversation

going, I asked brightly, 'Mother, what does "F——K" mean?' The effect was surprising. The Reverend Daniel choked, and ejected his teeth into his soup-plate, where with scarlet face he chased them round and round with his spoon. Mother said, 'Ask your father,' and I saw Father flash an unspoken retort back to Mother. Feeling that some explanation was called for, I added timidly, 'Someone has chalked it on our back gate, and I just wondered.'

After lunch Mother quietly said to me, 'That word is never used in polite society', whereupon I sponged it off the back gate. I did not ask Father; and it was several more years before a boy at school told me exactly what it meant. My reactions then were (a) 'Don't be disgusting!' (b) 'I don't believe a word of it', (c) 'I would never dream of doing such a thing!' Which only shows how wrong you can be.

It also shows how completely our family had succeeded (without conscious effort) in ignoring the whole subject of 'sex', now regarded by so many as the all-pervasive theme of their existence. We had our full share of parental love and were not as yet yearning for anything else. Father and Mother were obviously very happy together, but we never had any indication of how far the matter occupied their thoughts. We were not of course a family of Arcadian innocents; our schoolmates saw to that. But in those days most people felt that the physical expression of love was too private and precious a thing to be commercialised and devalued as it is now. It seems that my generation occupied roughly a middle position in the slow swing from Victorian prudery to present-day permissiveness. Some of us, it's true, might have preferred to join the fun at a rather later stage; but, alas, you get no choice.

Not long ago I came upon a sampler on which a little girl of eight had been induced to spend hours stitching, and presumably engraving on her own heart, the following axiom of 1826:

> Religion should our thoughts engage
> Amidst our youthful bloom.
> T'will fit us for declining age,
> And for the awful tomb.

We seem to have come a long way since then. And now whither? Or have we already attained the ultimate in morality, the best ever?

In the spring of 1911, King George V and Queen Mary came to stay at Edinburgh's royal palace of Holyrood. As Mother said,

One went again to make one's bow to Royalty. This time I wore an apricot satin dress, partly veiled in fine black georgette, with a black satin train borrowed from my sister-in-law. The highlight of this dress was a most lovely gold and coloured silk embroidered front for the bodice which I had brought from India; and with a bouquet of crimson roses it made a becoming ensemble.

When Queen Mary opened a new wing of the Elsie Inglis Hospital, being on the Committee I was one of those to receive her. One small girl presented her with a bouquet, and Helena was to have presented another to Princess Mary, and was very disappointed when at the last moment the young Princess was unable to come.

In early Summer we had a wedding at Drumearn when our faithful maid, Agnes, was married by my husband to a nice man who worked in the mines near Preston Pans, and Helena had her moment of excitement as her small bridesmaid.

Thus went the social whirl. But for Father a heavy task was in store. In April 1908 there had died one of the great figures of the Church of Scotland, Dr Archibald Hamilton Charteris, D.D., L.L.D., Professor of Biblical Criticism and Biblical Antiquities in the University of Edinburgh, Chaplain to Queen Victoria and King Edward, Dean of the Chapel Royal of Scotland, Moderator of the General

Assembly of 1892, and President of the Young Men's Guild of the Church of Scotland. The biography had been entrusted to Dr Graham, a skilled writer and missionary at Kalimpong, who took with him to India a vast multitude of letters; but overwork and poor health compelled him to abandon even the preliminary work. Mrs Charteris therefore appealed to father to undertake it, and Father, ever the willing horse, felt it his duty to accept. He had never written a book before, and there was three years' delay to be overtaken. He knew the risks to himself, but was not deterred. Soon packing cases arrived from India, and stacks of old letters in faded handwriting covered the study carpet, the shelves, and even monopolised the billiard table which the parents had installed for our use.

Father's plan was to produce a detailed and accurate biography, which would also 'throw much-needed light on recent Church history affecting the relations of the Church of Scotland with the other Presbyterian Churches'. This, with his legal background, he was uniquely fitted to do. Mother came to his help, as far as she was able. She bought an old typewriter and, learning as she went along, typed most of the rough draft at his dictation. She tells of the endless procession of facts, quotations and dates which had to be extracted and verified from those thousands of faded letters. It was often the fashion in the last century to write in both directions across the sheet. For a discursive writer this may have saved paper, but the reader of faded letters found it anything but helpful.

Father drove himself hard. The very sight of those stacks of letters, and the effort to remember even part of their contents, must at times have turned him giddy. Night after night we left him at his desk — 'Just an hour or two more.' Within a year the book was published; and had on the whole a good reception.

The title was inevitably ponderous: *The Life of the Very Reverend Archibald Hamilton Charteris D.D., LL.D., Professor of Biblical Criticism and Biblical Antiquities in the University of Edinburgh.* But most of the critics were kind. 'Dr Charteris has been fortunate in his biographer' (the *Scotsman*); 'Great literary skill, an instructive biography of a great churchman' (the *Glasgow Herald*); 'A classic work written in a fine spirit of moderation and Christian charity' (*Aberdeen Daily Journal*); 'With unflagging interest we have read this fascinating volume' (the *Primitive Methodist Leader*). And so on.

On the other hand the local paper of Dr Charteris's birthplace devoted no less than five editorial columns to hole-picking, and finished by saying, 'Mr Gordon sinks the dignity of biographer and historian to become the retailer of paltry gossip.' And the *Yorkshire Daily Observer* sourly observed, 'To speak of the tortuous ways of Mr Gladstone argues a perverted vision.'

Father's one little joke was a minor calamity. He had referred to the Church of Scotland monthly magazine, founded by Dr Charteris and partly printed on pink paper, as the *Ecclesiastical Pink 'Un*. Too late Father was to learn that the real *Pink 'Un* was a paper widely read by the racing fraternity, not for its spiritual content, but because its pink pages were covered with distinctly blue jokes. 'Deplorable', commented the critic of the *Athenæum*; and ruefully Father agreed. But he had given good measure. The cost to purchasers of this 500-page volume was only 10s. 6d. The cost to himself Father had yet to pay.

12
Kaleidoscope

When I was thirteen Mother decided it was time that the toughness of my Scottish education should be refined by the softer cultural influence of an English public school. At least that was the idea. After a comprehensive survey of the schools available, she selected Clifton, because the son of a Scottish Minister whom we knew was head of one of the houses and would help me to feel at home there. But things did not quite work out that way. The head of the house knew, and I myself soon became aware, that if it was known that he was looking after me, neither of us would ever live it down. So during my first term, which was also his last, we avoided each other like the plague, and I had to find my own feet in a strange new world. Mother did her best to help me at the outset. She took lodgings nearby, and it was a comfort to me to know I could slip in there once in a while and find much-needed reassurance.

167

That Clifton was a very different place from Merchiston I discovered on my first morning in chapel. During the prayers I leaned forward, as is sometimes the Scottish custom, but did not kneel on my knees like the rest. This also had the advantage of keeping my new black trousers off the dirty floor. Ever since Jenny Geddes threw her stool at the Bishop who was trying to force Charles I's English Prayer-book on a Scottish congregation, we of the Church of Scotland have secretly smiled at the obeisances and genuflections that seem so important to Anglican or Episcopalian worshippers. I recalled the old rhyme —

> Piscy, Piscy, Ah — men,
> Doon on yer knees, an' up agen!

My reverie was abruptly broken by a vicious poke on my behind with the point of an umbrella, and on turning round I saw a furious bearded face glaring at me from above a parson's dog-collar. 'Kneel down,' he hissed. 'Don't you poke me,' I retorted with indignation, pushing the umbrella away. And there the matter stayed; until at the end of the morning my form-master, a Scot with a sense of humour, called me to him and asked for my version of the stinging report that had reached him. I asked rather hotly if it was right that I should be forced to abandon the customs of the church of my fathers at the point of an umbrella. To which he replied, 'Laddie, you're in Rome now. In details that don't matter, it's as well to do as the Romans do.' Thereafter I conformed to the extent of leaning forward with one knee resting lightly against a clean hassock. The Church Militant relaxed. The umbrella slept in its sheath.

Two things at Clifton repelled me from the start — cold baths in winter, and pack-runs on the Downs. Each morning I went with others to the washroom, stood a bucket on a marble shelf, filled it to the brim with icy water, and up-ended it over my head. This Spartan ritual, relic of the

Victorian age, and the subsequent rub-down with a coarse towel, certainly did something for you, and I did my duty as required. It was only later that I was able to develop that flick of the wrist that flung the water in the air and enabled one to jump aside and avoid the full shock of the icy douche. But there was no avoiding the pack-runs on the Downs. Indeed, whippers-in with switches were there to see that there were no stragglers.

The good long-distance runners were those with thin sinewy legs and inexhaustible lungs. Being heavily built I found it difficult to keep up, and my progress across the Downs must have resembled that of an aged sheep with a dog at its heels. The situation was not made any more bearable by the ribald comments of Bristol residents walking there at their ease. The most depressing thing was that the running itself was devoid of either destination or purpose. Maintaining a breezy conversation, the pack-leaders would run a mile in one direction, then suddenly turn and run half a mile in another direction, then off again in a third direction, while I lumbered along behind trying to divine their next move and cut the corner. If the object of this aimless running was to develop self-mastery by forcing oneself to do something quite useless and uncongenial, one might surely have attained that object with less waste of energy by sitting on an Indian fakir's bed of nails. I mentioned this to Mother, saying I found the runs futile and exhausting; with which she agreed.

There was another ordeal which worried me even more, namely the New Boys' Concert. I was told it was the custom that a month after the term began an unofficial concert was held by the senior boys in the wash-room, at which each new boy was required to stand naked on a table and sing a song. The audience's reaction depended on how the song was put over. I could guess only too well what my reception would be, having never sung a solo song in my life. I went to a music shop and chose two songs: 'Love's garden of roses', which had a soulful-looking lady with a large bosom on the cover; and a comic song whose chorus went 'When Father papered the parlour, You couldn't see Pa for paste', which the music-shop man assured me was guaranteed to get a lot of laughs. We tried them on the piano in Mother's digs until I knew them both by heart. Yet the only thing I was sure of was that my rendering of either song, unaccompanied by any music, would be simply disastrous, and I was very worried at the prospect.

After ten days or so we both agreed it was time for Mother to go home, and I would get through the term as best I could. So she left. Next day my house-master sent for me and spoke very kindly. He asked how I liked the pack-runs, and I admitted I wished there was some other form of exercise. He said an hour's squash-rackets would do instead, and he would have my name taken off the pack-run list. My other fear, the New Boys' Concert, likewise found a solution. It simply did not take place.

How Mother had the nerve to confront my housemaster — for that is what I afterwards suspected — I don't know; but I was not the only new boy who was thankful for her intervention.

Before me is a letter, dated 1 January 1976, written by a distant cousin to Helena, which contains this passage: 'Olga was always so ready to help anyone in any way. I remember her saying to me, "When I die, I hope they will write on my tomb-stone — 'She did what she could!' " She was half-joking at the time, but it would really very well describe her.'

It goes without saying that Mother's interventions were always intended for the best. But sometimes the result was not too good. The year before I was sent to Clifton she happened to look down my throat and formed the opinion that all was not well. What she had seen were my tonsils. Normally she would have consulted Dr Carter. But this time she decided for herself that they should come out, and all that remained was to choose the surgeon. But there really was no choice about it. Mother had decided that the best man for the job was Mr John Wishart (an alias, of course), for he was a most devout Elder of the Church and would charge less than the usual fee. The fact that he was normally an abdominal specialist was ignored, though I remember that after he had looked down my throat, he did his best to get out of the assignment, but without success.

The operation was carried out in Father's dressing-room, and it was more than a week before I could swallow anything other than iced water, Brands' Essence, and peeled grapes. Years later, when Ted was an experienced doctor, he told me I was lucky to get away with it. Much of the back lining of my throat had been removed, and he had seen sprays of arterial blood on the walls of the dressing-room. This was deplorable, because what Mother had saved on Mr Wishart's fee had to be spent in redecorating the room.

When Mother launched me at Clifton she still retained her dream of bringing out her musical talent in me. She took me to a concert in Bristol where I incautiously showed great enthusiasm over the performance of the solo violinist. That was enough. In spite of my previous failure as a pianist, she determined to make a violinist of me. Fifteen pounds was spent on a violin, and four half-hour practices and one hour's lesson were required of me each week. For Mother's sake I endured this for five years, by which time my playing remained an ordeal alike for the listener and for myself, my theme song, appropriately, the 'Chanson Triste'. When I left school the violin was sold for £15, a surprisingly good price considering all it had undergone at my hands. But those hours were not entirely wasted. They helped me to appreciate music, so long as it was played by others.

Mother greatly approved of physical fitness, believing that it betokened success in the world. During Ted's last two years at Merchiston she watched nearly every rugger match, 'often wondering if my son *could* come out unscathed'. When he was given his 1st XV cap, she was very proud, especially as Merchiston was the champion Scottish school that year. It was bad luck that he injured his knee in the last match and never played rugger again. Golf then became his game, which he played into his eighties.

In 1912 he went to Cambridge to study medicine. This marked a further stage in our family break-up as our holidays no longer coincided, and thereafter the family magazine seldom appeared.

In February Father had his first stroke. On the previous day he had taken no less than four services, two of them as Chaplain to the Royal Scots regiment. Next morning Mother heard the sudden cry, 'Oh my head, my head!' Dr Carter prescribed absolute rest in a darkened room, with ice-packs. Father could see and speak, but he gave the wrong names to letters, and could neither read nor write. He was well recovered in a few months' time, though he could never work at his normal level again. But he fought a good fight against recurrent strokes during the seven years that remained to him.

By July he was well enough to accept an invitation to preach at an evening service held in the open air amid the lovely ruins of Dryburgh Abbey, where Sir Walter Scott lies buried. As this was in a sense his swan-song, let me quote his modest note of the occasion:

It was an exceptionally lovely summer evening, dry and warm, though the season was a very wet one. The large crowd which gathered in that exquisitely beautiful historic site influenced me in a high degree. Standing on the base of one of the old pillars nearly opposite the tomb of the immortal Wizard of the North, I began with a reference to a native of Duns, Thomas McCrie the historian, and his views on Christian Unity. I did not fail in letting the people hear, in that ruined temple made with hands, that we were ever looking up, through the rich glories of the

varied foliage and the gorgeous hues of transfigured clouds and
the declining sun, to that heaven

>Where high the Heavenly Temple stands,
>The House of God not made with hands.

I appealed in the words of the Great High Priest himself 'that
they all may be one', etc., and urged the Christian good of Scotland, and the needs of the great heathen or non-Christian World.

At the close several representatives of the ministry and members of other Churches expressed their agreement and sympathy
with the sentiments which had been expressed.

In the following year the University of Edinburgh conferred on him the Honorary Degree of Doctor of Divinity,
'for his varied and disinterested labours and especially for
his memorial of the notable life of Dr A. H. Charteris'. He
was also appointed Chaplain to the Edinburgh Garrison,
ranking as full Colonel, and awarded the Territorial
Decoration.

Further, he was appointed by the King to be Chaplain
of the Royal Company of Archers (King's Bodyguard for
Scotland). We all felt this really was something, for 'The
Archers' who had so impressed Mother at her first Court
had been founded in the time of Charles II, 'as an influen-
tial body of Noblemen and Gentlemen who met for the
purpose of encouraging the Noble and Useful Recreation
of Archery'. In 1822 they were given the title of the
'King's Body Guard for Scotland', and Queen Victoria
limited the number of officers to twenty-eight, each
appointment to be subject to the Sovereign's personal
approval.

Everything possible was done to ensure that the appearance of this ancient and distinguished corps should be
properly impressive. The dark green uniform, Tam-o'-
Shanter hat with its immense eagle-plume and silver badge,
the long-bow and quiver, and the great dagger (or sword,
for an officer) produced an effect almost as imposing as

that of the Cock-of-the-North himself. It was too sad to find that the designer of the uniform had decreed that the Chaplain, since he represented One who was 'meek and lowly in heart', should be totally disarmed. Father was not even allowed a feather in his hat. In fact so plain was his uniform that on state occasions he felt compelled to travel to and from Holyrood Palace in a closed cab to avoid being mistaken for a Tram Inspector.

An incident was recorded at the time by Lord Lothian which well illustrates Queen Victoria's concern for her subjects, especially her soldiers. It concerns the famous 'Wet Review' of 1881, when on a bitterly cold day the rain poured down throughout the day and the following night, saturating the troops, and causing casualties from exposure and subsequent pneumonia. The Queen, sitting in her open carriage, observed that the Duke of Abercorn, Captain-General of her Body Guard, despite his advanced years and high office, was suffering with the rest from the chilling deluge. She summoned the Duke of Connaught, who was mounted at the side of her carriage, and told him to tell the Duke to put on his greatcoat.

The Duke of Connaught obeyed, but brought back the reply that His Grace could not think of thus protecting himself in Her Majesty's presence.

On hearing this the Queen said to His Royal Highness: 'Ride over and tell the Duke that I *command* him to put on his greatcoat.'

The Duke of Connaught delivered this second message to the Captain-General, who said: 'To tell you the truth, Sir, we do not possess greatcoats; but I did not like to confess this when you first made known Her Majesty's kind wish to me.'

The Duke galloped back to the royal carriage and explained matters to the Queen who, without further comment, turned in her seat and asked one of the kilted attendants behind her to produce her brown Shetland shawl. The Queen then held it out to the Duke of Connaught and said: 'Take this to the Duke, and tell him to wrap it round his shoulders at once!' The story unhappily ends there; for Lord Lothian was unable to say what the Captain-General did on receipt of the Queen's shawl.

Next day came the message – 'The Queen desires me to inquire whether any of the Royal Archers has seriously suffered from their lengthened exposure to the very inclement weather of yesterday. She would greatly regret if it were so, remembering to what inconvenience many gentlemen must have been put in forming her Body-Guard.' Royal, indeed!

That year the family spent Christmas in London, and among memorable sights I recall the lurid effect of road-flares in a pea-soup fog at Marble Arch. Of historical importance was the appearance of Ethel Levy in *Hullo, Miss Rag-time!* for it signalised the invasion of Europe by syncopated rhythm from America. Everyone's toes were tapping to such songs as 'Alexander's Ragtime Band', 'Oh, you beautiful doll' and 'Hitchy Koo'.

When the family went off to the Drury Lane Pantomime they had to leave me in bed with a high fever from a septic throat. I was deaf in one ear, with bits of tonsils and adenoids still surviving to cause recurring trouble. Altogether my throat was in such a state that Mother decided to make a final attempt to straighten it out. This time she selected Mark Hovell who, she told me, was one of the throat specialists called in to operate on the Kaiser's father who had (with hushed voice) cancer of the throat, from which he died; and she lent me a book all about it, with diagrams. I of course concluded that this was her way of gently breaking it to me that I too had cancer of the throat, and secretly prepared myself as best I could for a ghastly end. But Mark Hovell, for all his sinister name, turned out to be a quiet capable little man, and in due course he did what he could to tidy up the wreckage left by his two predecessors. Neither he nor Mother can have known what it meant to me to be told after several weeks' suspense that all would now be well. Some weeks later an entry appeared in the pocket-diary which I had started to keep at school. 'Throat much better. Mother says she is now doctoring Fifi, who has worms.' Fifi was her new French bull-dog, to whom I was thankful to yield place as the focus of medical interest.

It was a title which Fifi did not hold for long. In January 1914 Father had another stroke and again lost his power of reading, and for some weeks had to be carefully nursed. However, he struggled gamely back to partial recovery.

In 1914 we spent our summer holidays at St Fillan's, on Loch Earn, a few miles west of Monzievaird. One Sunday at the parish church, the Minister at the end of his sermon was seen to be failing. Father, who knew only too well what was happening to him, left our pew and before Mother could stop him climbed up the pulpit stairs and helped the Minister down and into the vestry. He then returned and finished the service in place of his stricken colleague. One must bear in mind that at that time doctors could hardly measure blood-pressure, let alone control it, and their only 'treatment' was to advise the patient to lead a quiet life. I thought little of the incident at the time; but now I realise that, weakened and brain-damaged as he was, Father was risking his life to help a stranger. And all he got for it was a scolding from Mother; a gentle scolding, for her written comment was 'mercifully all went well'.

On 4 August 1914, Germany having invaded Belgium and France in violation of joint treaties ('the scrap of paper'), Britain declared war on her. At the end of our month at St Fillan's, Ted rejoined us at Drumearn. He had tried to join up, but was told that he should continue his studies and qualify as a doctor. They were taking no one under eighteen, so I had another two years to do at Clifton. Helena was sent to a girls' boarding school in England;

and thus by mid-September, all the birds of our nest were, so to speak, on the wing.

But before Ted left for London there was a terrible flutter. To use Mother's own phrase from long ago, 'Cupid's dart' had been busy! She first discovered this when, on entering Ted's bedroom in his absence, she found on the dressing-table a letter in feminine handwriting. The envelope had been opened; she drew out the letter and read it. The full gravity of the situation broke on her when she realised that the lady who wrote it was on the stage and that Teddy, her own son, was intending to marry her.

Mother reacted with every fibre of her being. Indeed Aunt Ellen herself could hardly have done better. She confronted Teddy with the letter. She told him he was to have nothing more to do with the girl; that if the situation became known it would kill Father; and that Teddy was not even to acknowledge the receipt of the letter. If he persisted, his allowance would be discontinued. This final sanction was a very strong one, as Teddy depended wholly on Mother for his livelihood and the cost of his medical studies. Whether, if driven to the point, Mother would have carried out her threat may be doubted. She had always been indulgent, especially to her eldest son, the apple of her eye. But, like her forebears, she was sure she knew best; and the threat remained.

Ted took me into his confidence and introduced me, hoping perhaps that I might help to bridge the gap between the girl and us. She was petite and lively, with an open face like a flower. She smelt like a flower, too. But as I had never met such an attractive girl before, there was little I could do for him. Mother sat tight, and the end of it was that in a few months' time the girl saw it was hopeless, and married another fellow whose family ties were less strict. After that I rarely saw my brother, and so I never knew how deeply he was affected. But another thirteen years were to pass before he married a charming wife, who incidentally bore a close resemblance to his first love.

In times gone by the Gordons were noted for their pride. In our family, though we have nothing much to be proud about, a streak of independence or cussedness sometimes still appears. The incident I have described, so humiliating to my brother, certainly brought it out in me; and I determined that Mother should know nothing of my love affairs until I was 'of independent means'. I too had to wait thirteen unlucky years, with some heartbreaks, before the way was clear. Things, they say, are easier now thanks to the Welfare State. Yet the suicide rate goes up. Very strange.

Once more the Aunts impinged on Mother's life, for although they were not short of great-nephews or great-nieces, they knew Mother was the one to be relied on. This time Aunt Sophy, the taller and younger of the two, had caught a chill which developed into pneumonia. She was seventy-five, and although no one went so far as to say so openly, it was generally felt that her time had come.

Mother arranged for a nurse to look after Father and set off by train for Tunbridge Wells. On arrival there she found the Aunt's condition very grave. Whether it was that Mother feared she would be caught unprepared, or whether she had absorbed the Merchiston School motto, 'Ready, aye ready', one cannot tell; but first thing next morning she hurried off with Aunt Liza to a costumier where they were fitted out in deep mourning of the very latest fashion; thence to the undertakers, where all the necessary arrangements were provisionally made. Only one point remained in doubt. How *long* was Aunt Sophy? They returned home and Mother, while tactfully engaging in sympathetic conversation with Moribund Aunt, stealthily plied her tape-measure along the side of the bed. All they could do now was to wait.

Late in the afternoon of the following day the doctor called again. He examined the old lady, and then broke the news that the end could not be far off. If available, he suggested, a little alcohol might ease her condition, though it could hardly affect the outcome. Aunt Eliza recalled that she had been keeping a half-bottle of champagne for some possible celebration. She fetched it from the cellar. Mother with difficulty opened it. They raised Aunt Sophy a little and induced her to take a sip. There was a long pause. The Aunt with the faintest gesture indicated she would try another sip. And a third. Then in a sepulchral voice she said, 'Draw down the blind!' This was not, as one might have supposed, a Suitable Last Word. It signified that she felt it was immodest to allow the neighbours to see her in night attire, drinking champagne in bed. As it was, she recovered and lived for another fifteen years, leaving Mother and Aunt Eliza to pack up their fashionable mourning 'weeds' in camphor-wood boxes.

13
Requiem for Father

1916; and time now for the war to blow our family life, with so many others, to the winds.

Ted was at St Bartholomew's Hospital, soon to qualify and join the Navy as a Temporary Surgeon-Lieutenant. I was leaving Clifton for the Royal Military Academy, Woolwich, aiming at a commission in the Field-gunners.

Clifton had done a lot for me; given me friendships, loyalty, a Classical Education, and a sharpened games-sense which during my last two years had earned me a place in the school team at football and cricket, and the captaincy of the 1st XI in my last term. After a nine months' crash course at Woolwich, Mother might have watched her second son at the passing-out parade. With glinting sword 'at the carry' and cap-peak down on his nose, he was marching round at the head of the column, humming the rude version of 'Colonel Bogey', and inwardly as thrilled as in the Monzievaird nursery. But Drumearn was far away; and somehow Mother never found time to repeat her first visit to Clifton.

During the summer of 1917 I spent two months in and out of many of the best shell-holes around Hell-Fire Corner; and then surprisingly survived the first six weeks of that glutinous inferno later to be known as 'Passchendaele'. Some much-needed light relief was supplied in correspondence with Ted who, on hearing where I was, sent me some tablets of morphia. The gift, though well-meant, started a train of thought which I could not afford; so I trod them into the mud. In return I sent him some indigestion tablets, for the poor chap was on a prolonged cruise in the sunny Adriatic where his chief responsibility lay in selecting the wines for the cruiser's wardroom.

Then I went south to Bapaume for that greatest of all (German) offensives in March 1918; and finally at Meteren, after Haig's 'backs-to-the-wall' message, I was caught by a German field-gun shell, aimed at me from only 600 yards away.

Now Mother comes in.

Vividly can I remember Friday, April 14th, when a telegram arrived saying Huntly was seriously wounded in the chest. In order to minimise alarm, I told my husband that the boy was wounded and we might be thankful he was out of the firing line. However two days later word came saying, 'Dangerously ill come at once' and further War Office instructions. Owing to the retreat, and re-inforcements being rushed across the Channel, visits by relatives were then limited to life-or-death cases only. With only a few hours to arrange everything I was off by the night train to London facing the possible death of my helpless husband from shock and of my sorely wounded son. It was an agonising position; in which Helena, who was at home for the Easter holidays, was a great help and consolation.

I reached the Hospital at Boulogne and probably helped to bring Huntly back to life, as the nurses had hardly been able to keep him going through the night. He had been shot through the back and lung and legs with fragments from a bursting shell, and only his young and strong physique and the goodness of God brought him through that, and the three months of septicaemia that followed. I was allowed to stay for a fortnight, and had to leave him unconscious after one of several operations to try to trace a small fragment in his lung that was causing the pain and abscesses.

In August, I was brought back to London, to a nursing-home in Bruton Street; and spent some happy hours in a wheelchair in the summerhouse in Berkeley Square; thence to an Officers' Convalescent Home in North Berwick, a lovely mansion called by happy chance 'Carle Kemp', the Camp of the Young Men. It was next to our Strathearn Lodge, by then in other hands. There the summer breezes and seaside air gave back to me and a dozen other young men something of our former health; though to tell the truth there wasn't much bounce left in any of us. While there, I was pensioned off to the Regular Army Retired List; and found myself on the shelf before I had even come of age.

But before the Camp of the Young Men broke up we celebrated the Armistice. It was an occasion when feelings long frozen began to thaw, and silent tears of relief and heartbreak mingled with the champagne provided by our generous hostess. And ten days later from the front lawn we watched — hardly believing our eyes — the long procession of the surrendering German High Seas Fleet; seventy warships steaming slowly up the Firth of Forth under the watchful guns of the Royal Navy.

Mother had rented a small house by the shore in the East Bay of North Berwick, which Father had known so well as a boy. Many happy hours he had spent there with his brothers playing around the Armchair Rock; and now it pleased him to sit in his wheelchair in the sunshine and revive old memories. And there Mother, with the help of

Helena and a kindly Scottish nurse-companion, did what they could to enliven his last days. He was by then almost helpless, unable to read or write or even to speak clearly, yet fully conscious. His limitations he bore patiently, and with never a word of complaint. He had so longed to see the war through to victory, and the Union of the Scottish Churches assured. Both these wishes had been fulfilled, and now he was ready to be gone.

The last occasion when our family were all together was when Ted came up from London for a weekend and joined in discussing my future. At first I had no interest in any future. Then I began to realise that man must work or starve. When I was a boy — quite a time ago that seemed — Uncle John had kindly suggested that I should join his firm on the Stock Exchange and perhaps someday become a partner. I had asked Father what the Stock Exchange did, and he had replied, 'Licensed gambling'. We agreed that moneymaking was a sordid business and one should look to the professions. So a non-committal answer had been sent to Uncle John. Too late now to reopen it. Uncle John was dead.

War had disqualified me for three of the professions, the Army, the Navy, the Church. The doctors had told me to take life very quietly, and that seemed to exclude the hard concentration of the legal profession. So the last choice was medicine. Ted said it was a good life, and painted a rosy picture of me leading a relaxed and social existence on the Côte d'Azur, ministering sympathetically to the trifling ailments of rich old ladies whom he would send me from London, and whom (if they survived my attentions) I could subsequently send back to him. It seemed a promising line. I sent for a scalpel and a preserved dogfish, this being the customary first step in studying the anatomy of rich old ladies. Subsequently I joined Ted at Bart's Hospital.

It was in early June 1919 that Father died. My brother and I came up from London in uniform to join Mother and

Helena. Many ministerial friends and elders were gathered in the sunshine at the Dean Cemetery, where his coffin covered with Gordon ivy was lowered into the grave where he had laid to rest his little son Arthur twenty years before. His oldest friend, dear Dr Russell of the silver locks and snowy beard, 'closed with the Benediction'.

As I mentioned in the Introduction, Father's background and interests differed so much from mine that, spending most of every year at school in England, I found it impossible to bridge the gap. What I have been able to write about him is little more than the close-up impressions of a boy too young to assess his qualities in any depth. But I now offer two assessments which may be of interest; one critical, the other generous.

The first appeared shortly after his death in the *Edinburgh Academy Chronicle*, his old school magazine; and it has something of the astringent tone of a school report, in welcome contrast to the usual obituary theme of 'Nil Nisi Bonum'.

Arthur Gordon was at first intended for the solicitor branch of his father's profession, but he forsook the Law for the Gospel, and became a student for the Ministry. His career in the Church was distinguished, but not very eventful, and it was interrupted and brought to a premature close by indifferent health. A most diligent and devoted pastor, who never slacked or spared himself, he was generally beloved by his people. Modest and unselfish, he was the kindest and most helpful of counsellors, but if by any chance there was some misunderstanding, a certain nervous and reticent obstinacy of temperament made smoothing over difficult. Perhaps his marvellous memory had something to do with the occasional implacability which was the only blemish in a singularly fine pastoral character.

To a certain extent Arthur Gordon disappointed the hopes that were entertained of him in the days when he was a senior student and the leader of the Conservative party in the University of Edinburgh. Partly owing to his social and political influence, but largely owing to his own ability and enthusiasm, he had come to be regarded at the time of his licence as the young Marcellus of the Scottish Church. But this expectation was not wholly fulfilled. He faded as a public speaker, and in his later years he was a stranger to the platform and rarely intervened in debate. . . . His sermons were too long to be popular, and there was a tendency to that over-elaboration which is sometimes hard to distinguish from prolixity, acquired perhaps during his legal training.

It was as a student of Scottish Church History in the nineteenth century that Gordon outshone all his contemporaries in his Church. He had mastered this subject from beginning to end, he was a mine of information upon it, and he was constantly of assistance to more prominent, if less learned, leaders of the Church. His interest was probably first aroused when he assisted his father, then Lord Advocate, in connection with the Patronage Abolition Act of 1874. In connection with this matter young Gordon was brought into touch with Disraeli, whose friendship with his father was perhaps the most potent influence in inducing the Government to promote the measure. It would be difficult to conceive of three men more different in every way than Benjamin Disraeli, Edward Strathearn Gordon, and Archibald Hamilton Charteris; but these were the three influences which moulded young Gordon and made him the minister of the Church best versed in public affairs; and — family affection apart — it would be hard to say for which of the three he felt the greatest veneration. His name, however, will always be associated with the last, for his Life of Professor Charteris is the monument to Arthur Gordon's memory, embodying, as it does, the inner and authentic history of the great popular revival of the Church of Scotland in the last forty years of the nineteenth century.

Dr Gordon had been quite laid aside for some time, and his last years were clouded by distressing illness patiently borne. The friends who gathered in the Dean Cemetery to lay him beside his father all felt that it was well that the same kind voice that called the young apprentice from the office desk to a life of devoted service had now at last called him home.   C. N. J.

The other was not so much an assessment as a warm-hearted tribute from the Reverend David Robertson. We first knew David as a boy in Father's Bible Class at Monzie-vaird, whose mother did the washing at the Manse. He was a boy of such promise that Father took especial care to help him and kept up with him throughout his life. We asked him to dedicate Father's memorial tablet in Monzie-vaird church, and this is what he said on that occasion:

It is very difficult for me to say all I would wish to say about one whose kindness and goodness I can never, never forget. Dr Gordon was ever my ideal of what a Minister ought to be: and much that I learned from him in the early days of his ministry at Monzievaird remains with me to this day, and has been of incalculable help to me.

It was, as you know, through the influence of his teaching that I am in the position I now occupy. He was always so sympathetic, so modest, so true. The Church has lost one of her ablest and most distinguished Ministers, and those of us who knew him intimately and who received inspiration and help from his life and ministry feel that we have indeed lost the truest and best friend we ever had.

In the preparation of his young communicants, he was faithful and tender; he set great store by the opportunities such a time afforded, and nothing rejoiced him more than to find in the hearts of his young people evidence of grace. How I treasure the memory of those Monzievaird days when he used frequently to visit my Mother's house — and how we always looked forward to seeing him, so much did we esteem him and love him.

A keen patriot, the soldiers' welfare lay close to his heart; he was chaplain for many years to the 4th Royal Scots, and also to the Royal Company of Archers (the King's Bodyguard for Scotland).

In 1912 there appeared his biography of Dr Charteris, which has been widely read and is a work of great value, being not only a record of the character and achievements of that eminent divine, but also a full history of the revival of Church life and the development and organisation of Church work from the time of the Disruption to modern days. His old University set the seal of its approbation on his work by conferring the honorary degree of Doctor of Divinity upon him in 1913. But that year saw him enfeebled in health. He had taxed his frame too severely in labours manifold; yet though his strength declined in succeeding years, he was able to plead for the Church's work in his own skilled and gracious way. Never once did he complain except to say that he was no longer of any use, for he had ever found his truest joy in unselfish service.

The late Dr Wallace Williamson, one of his chief friends, conveyed to him the sympathy of the College of Moderators, and there is little doubt that if he had been spared he would have been called to occupy the Chair of the General Assembly, the highest honour the Church can bestow. Such recognition greatly touched and cheered him. But his spirit was weary, and soon after he passed peacefully away after long days of suffering patiently borne; and was laid to rest in the Dean Cemetery, Edinburgh on the 14th June 1919. To me there was no other Minister like Dr Gordon, and I shall treasure his memory, his influence, and his example to the end of my life.

14
The Long, Long Trail

Mother was now left on her own, with Helena. Drumearn, being too big for them, was eventually sold with much of its furniture. As Mother dispassionately recorded. 'My husband and I used to talk about the future when I should no longer have his company; and we agreed that as my elderly relatives all lived in the South it would be my duty to return to the land from whence I came.' Duty? I wonder. That last phrase has an Old Testament ring. If I am not mistaken Mother was thinking of the story of Naomi and Ruth. When the grieving heart sees life closing in towards its end, it longs instinctively to return to the memories and scenes of childhood. And so, her Scottish adventure now over, she looked south to England once more. 'Our first resting-place, therefore, was Tunbridge Wells, to be near the old Aunts.' Tunbridge Wells; which once before had been her first resting-place, at the end of a little girl's long voyage from India. And still the old Aunts were there, providing, like a pair of ancient yew-trees, an assurance of continuity, almost of immortality, in a changing world.

However, three months' rest in the shade of the Aunts was long enough to generate an urge for travel. So off went Mother again, this time with Helena, to Paris, Milan, Rome, Naples, Sorrento, Pompeii, Florence; and then East-bourne, Ilfracombe and a weekend with a nephew at Oxford. But sometime they would have to settle some-where; and recalling her days at Wimbledon she bought a cosy little house at the foot of the hill, which she re-named 'Struan' after Father's first parish.

Fortunately Struan was only a few minutes' walk from the Pres-byterian Church, whose minister at that time was Rev. Duncan Macgregor. We soon made friends with him and his wife. It was a God-send to me, as it helped to break the fall of leaving Scotland and Presbyterianism; and his services and prayers so reminded me of my husband. During that time Mr Macgregor received his D.D. from Edinburgh University; and it was a great satisfaction to me to pass on to him my husband's cap and hood, which had only been worn at his capping in the McEwan Hall in 1913.

Ted by now was busy as junior partner in a London West-end practice. Soon he was on his own and steadily making a good reputation, especially among celebrities from the USA. He married, and after some years presented Mother with her first grandson. He outlived Mother and his smooth-running life-story must have given almost as much satisfaction to her as it did to him.

While we are at it, let us dispose of her second son's life-story, which on the face of it was a less satisfactory affair. It would no doubt be true to say that the effects of the war made it difficult for him to settle down, though one must not forget Shakespeare's ruthless observation, 'The fault, dear Brutus, is not in our stars, but in ourselves, that we are underlings.' At any rate for three years after the war Huntly slogged away at his medical studies among a crowd of schoolboys, passing his exams without delay. Then, no longer able to endure the frustration of an empty pocket and the ineffectiveness of medical treatment in the days before antibiotics, he landed a good job with a leading oil company. This took him unexpectedly to China, where after three years he was caught up in a wave of anti-foreign outbreaks instigated by Russian Communists; and narrowly escaped from an enraged mob who attacked him at a remote up-country station. Returning home in the late 1920s he began again to look for suitable work. But work of any sort was hard to get when nearly two million unemployed were desperately looking for it.

So he was lucky to find a bread-and-butter job with a public service corporation; where, after a further seven despairing years as an underling, he became head of the Industrial Welfare department and was at last of independent means. He married happily, in time to give Mother her first grandchild (a daughter), thus winning this particular contest by a short head from his brother. Four years later his first son was born. At the end of the Second World War, however, this marriage fell apart, without dishonour on either side. Seven years later he married again, a war-widow, clear-eyed, with a seven-year-old son. Two more sons were born and all five have turned out well. So, after a shaky start and some rough weather, Huntly's life-story came right in the end, bringing mutual happiness, in which Mother also shared in her latter days. And as this story is chiefly about her, that will be enough about her sons.

Struan was not only conveniently close to the Presbyterian Church but to the Wimbledon Tennis Club in Worple Road, where on four or five open grass courts, with some modest seating accommodation for spectators, the World Championships were annually held. That glorious summer of 1920 witnessed the arrival of a tennis prodigy, Mlle Suzanne Lenglen, who surprised everyone by proving most emphatically that agile youth in short skirts, gym-shoes, and a ballet dancer's style, could beat elderly ladies of long experience in long skirts and long-laced boots. Her performance was thought to have something of the miraculous, until persistent questioning by reporters revealed that her father had made her practise throughout her childhood until she could land four out of five drives on a postcard. Some people were old-fashioned enough to deplore such unremitting practice because it reduced the element of luck that added so much to the enjoyment of the game. But you cannot resist change, and thus were born the grim-faced contests of today.

But, tennis apart, Struan as a residence had its disadvantages too.

> We discovered too late that on one side of our little garden was a Y.M.C.A. Meeting-Room, and across the road some other religious conventicle. On hot Sunday afternoons hymns blared at us simultaneously from open windows to right and to left, and we could get no peace. To live there continuously would be impossible.

So they moved to a more secluded house in Guildford.

In 1922 Mother took a further opportunity of doing homage to King George and Queen Mary. At a drawing-room at Buckingham Palace she presented two debutantes, Helena and a friend.

> Being still in mourning I wore a black satin dress of former days, to which I added a train of black faille shot with gold. Helena had a pretty pale turquoise blue georgette dress, veiled with silk net striped with gold bugle beads, and a belt made from the Indian embroidery that I had used on a previous occasion. The train was gold embroidered net, lined with turquoise blue.

Their Majesties could hardly fail to be impressed. No doubt the friend wore something more than a broad smile, but precise details are lacking.

I myself, being by this time in the interior of China, was no longer in a position to follow Mother and Helena in their travels about Europe, and now that I have time to read her account of them, I do so with admiration and astonishment. She evidently regarded travel much as Robert Louis Stevenson, when he said, 'For my part, I travel not to go anywhere, but to go. I travel for travel's sake. The great affair is to move.' Yet, though she did not say so, I fancy that abroad her thoughts would often be winging back to Father, remembering their romantic meeting, and their honeymoon in Northern Italy. As it would be wearisome to punctuate this narrative by listing their travels, year by year, as they took place, I shall compress them into a list resembling a tourist's holiday catalogue, to be perused or skipped as the reader wishes.

In 1922, Mother and Helena spent a month in Sicily, at Palermo, Taormina, Girgenti, Syracuse and other places of interest in Greek history. Then she records that in 1924 'we two in company with Reginald Constant and Charlie Cooper (cousins) paid a short visit to the Italian lakes, where I renewed the memories of those happy days in 1892 when I met the two Scottish strangers in the train at Menaggio.' Later there were two winter-sports holidays at Engelberg; a trip with poor cousin Daisy ('Miss Constant') to the Norwegian Fjords; a Hellenic cruise from Venice by Dubrovnik, Athens, and Rhodes to Constantinople. And there was a month in Guernsey with visits to Paris and Brussels. And another in Rome, Capri, Portofino, and Alassio.

In 1934 they travelled to Palestine where they visited many places which had become familiar through her reading of the Bible and from Father's descriptions. Their destination was of course Jerusalem, in time for the dedication of the newly-built Scottish Church, erected by Scots in all parts of the world as a memorial to their countrymen who had fallen in the Great War.

It was a building of singular beauty and simplicity, full of Scottish sentiment. The seating consisted of oak arm-chairs each donated by a Scottish parish. The nearest I could get to Monzievaird, which small parish had not donated a chair, was one with the name of Crieff on its brass plate, but it was really with thoughts of Monzievaird that I sat there through the Sunday evening service.

On our way south we halted at Capernaum by the Lake of Galilee, and going down to the water's edge I filled two medicine bottles with Jordan water to bring home for Gordon baptisms. When my husband, as a bachelor, had visited Palestine he had brought back a bottle of Jordan water as a souvenir, and his first son was baptised with it. The water I procured seemed none too pure, and many times did I boil and strain it to keep it reasonably fresh. It was used on our return for the baptism of Huntly's daughter Ann; also Teddy's boy, Alastair, who was born nine months later, on which occasion the verger had the effrontery to describe it as rather smelly.

We drove along the lakeside to Tiberias, where we lunched on fish from the lake, and thereafter by the water's edge thought of the scenes described in the New Testament on and beside those same waters of holy memory. It was a moving experience to visit Jacob's well, one of the few places that had remained unchanged since Bible times, and to hear in imagination Christ's talk with the woman of Samaria. And when the little old monk let down a light into the depths, saying 'The well is deep' (John IV: 11) one's heart was too full for words.

We visited Gordon's Calvary, so called because General Gordon had been the first in recent years to recognise it as Golgotha, the place of the skull. The configuration of the rock had an un-mistakeably skull-like appearance, as so well shown in the photograph my husband sent me before our engagement. Also the empty tomb in the garden close by, in which only one of the three burial places had been completed, closely following the Bible description.

It was in the late 1920s that Mother's long-lived relations began to vanish from the scene. First to go was Uncle

George, who had lived in retirement from the Indian Medical Service for more than half of his ninety years. Aunt Ellen waited only a few months in her Eastbourne drawing-room before following him. Mother began to wonder how much longer it would be before the old Aunts began to think of moving on. She felt a special responsibility for them which could not be exercised from a distance. Therefore either she and Helena must move to Tunbridge Wells, or the Aunts must be moved to Guildford. She chose the latter course, rented a house nearby, found a charming Irish couple to look after them and carried out the move. Their furniture, including in particular the ferocious portrait of their Waterloovian progenitor, handed down by their mother, was arranged as it had been in their home; and it was hoped that under these circumstances the fact that they had been moved might almost have escaped their notice. But that hope was in vain. Aunt Eliza, the senior one, suddenly began to show signs of ageing, and after a short period of being bed-ridden just before her ninetieth birthday, she slipped peacefully away. Neither of them had realised the death of their brother George, three years before; so Aunt Sophy was left wandering around and asking 'Where's Eliza?' Mother sympathetically commented that the pangs of separation mercifully seem to grow less as one descends into the last valley.

Next to go, and most deeply mourned of all, was dear Aunt Lena. After a short fortnight's illness, and attended by Mother in her last hours, she died in Eastbourne and was buried beside her beloved husband under the pines in Bournemouth. I here pay my last tribute to her habit of doing things in the grand manner. In 1918 when war-time sweets were few and of inferior quality, she took the trouble to arrange for a representative from Charbonnel & Walker of Bond Street, the Rolls-Royce of chocolate-makers, to call on me at the nursing-home in Bruton Street and ensure that my wants in that direction were fully supplied, and at her own expense.

Finally it was Aunt Sophy's turn. She succeeded in clocking up ninety years, and then passed suddenly away. Both sisters had particularly asked for a full-dress funeral, in which horses with purple draperies and nodding black plumes should be a leading feature. But those days had long gone by and it was in a small cortège of well-sprung Daimlers that each in turn was borne from Guildford, home to Tunbridge Wells. I expect Mother wore her camphor-fragrant black garments of fifteen years before; but to tell the truth I forgot to ask her. Hail and Farewell then to the old Aunts! In 1930 there cannot have been many people who could say, 'My father fought at Waterloo.'

At the end of the 1920s there was a great increase in motor traffic, particularly on the Portsmouth road, when during the summer a never-ending stream of sailors on leave came roaring by on motor-bikes throughout the night to the exasperation of the residents. At that time Helena, having taken a secretarial course, wanted to get a job in London. It therefore suited both her and Mother that the house should be sold and they should move into the capital. For a time the noise on the Portsmouth Road deterred buyers, but in due course Mother's Guardian Angel (who on the whole had had a busy life) came along with a couple of ladies who were almost stone-deaf. They bought the property on the spot under the impression that many others were about to snap it up.

Throughout the 1930s Helena worked on the staff of the Ascot office, with the delicate task of weeding out the applications of those who had been divorced, and gently breaking it to them that only those whose marital record, if any, was classed as stainless could enter the Royal Enclosure.

Mother was by now well into her sixties, and developing a philosophical attitude to life with its ups and downs. This was as well; because a stranger, choosing a moment when her Guardian Angel was otherwise occupied, 'entered the flat and relieved me of all my jewellery, which I had carefully locked in my jewel-case and hidden in my linen drawer. I had some quite nice things of sentimental value, including a half-hoop diamond bracelet, a wedding present from Lady Gordon, and other valuable gifts from my husband. Of course they were never traced and I got very little compensation. Gradually I have become accustomed to losses of various kinds, and have learned that it is not wise to allow oneself to become too sentimental over possessions. After all we are only Pilgrims, and it is best to travel light.'

Her Guardian Angel must have taken this lapse very much to heart, for (glancing ahead for a moment to 1940 and Hitler's bombing raids) Mother felt a strong urge to move into the country beforehand. '*Mercifully* one was guided along those lines, as six months later our block of flats had a direct hit and five dwellers in the basement were killed.' Which shows that the guidance of Guardian Angels was personal and strictly defined. Those of us who were Hitler's targets in London at that time will remember that point of view. How often did we not gaze upwards at an approaching 'doodle-bug' and, assessing the moment when it would pass over and demolish the *next* street, exclaim with a sigh of satisfaction, 'That one's all right!'

Some years before the outbreak of the Second World War, Mother had used the money from the sale of her Guildford house to build a weekend country home among the pine trees on Crooksbury Ridge near Farnham. It had a superb view over undulating ridges of heathlands to Hindhead, several miles away. We named it 'Heatherbrae', as it reminded us so much of the Scottish Highlands. Looking ahead in the months preceding the war, Mother had also foreseen that Heatherbrae would be useful as a sanctuary for various old friends who would be better out of London when the crisis broke.

Chief of these was Aunt Aggie, Father's youngest sister, aged 80, who lived in a top-floor flat in Westminster. I had a special feeling for this Aunt, because although she rarely met us she always sent us a five-shilling postal order at Christmas time. This useful gift only varied once, when Aunt Aggie must have felt that something less impersonal would be appreciated. In that year I received a large clock-work ladybird, which crawled around on our dining-room carpet in a most lively fashion. How was she to know that the small boy she had in mind was already a full-grown soldier shortly leaving for the Western Front? And now, twenty-two years later I was to arrange for her removal to Heatherbrae and safety.

I reconnoitred the position cautiously, visiting her several times in a casual way. With the waywardness of the old, she took me for my brother Ted, who never found time to call on her, and in fact had not seen her for years. Each time I left, her last words were, 'Thank you so much for calling, and remember me to your brother Huntly. Such a pity I never see him nowadays.' It was useless to explain, as she did not listen.

A few days before war broke out I called to make final plans for her removal. Aunt Aggie was in bed with a cold. She sat propped up on pillows, a little shaky, her scanty fair hair gathered into two wisps, each tied with pale blue ribbon, matching her eyes — so like Father's. I gently opened up our proposal to her, telling her that any day now German bombers might arrive overhead and rain down destruction on the capital. Even if her flat was not hit, there was danger from fire and flying glass, and I pointedly glanced up at the large glass skylight overhead. Then I explained that we would have a comfortable car ready, and in less than two hours she would be snugly housed with Mother miles out of harm's way. And finally I mentioned that there might not be much time left.

She heard me out in silence, trembling slightly. Then looking me straight in the eye, she spoke. 'As I understand it, Teddy, you are suggesting that I should move from here. [She paused.] But, for a Gordon to turn her back on the enemy — No! That would never do.' There was no more to be said; and soon afterwards I left, thankful that as far as Aunt Aggie was concerned it was Teddy, not Huntly, who had dared to make so craven a suggestion.

I passed the problem back to Mother, as I was then busy with the evacuation of some of London's children. Before a month of Hitler's 'phoney war' had passed, Aunt Aggie found her own solution by slipping quietly away in her sleep.

When in 1940 the Battle of Britain began and occasional German bombers strayed into the skies of outer Surrey, Mother who (to use her dramatic phrase) was 'holding the fort at Heatherbrae', began to make her own arrangements to meet the possibility of invasion. She cashed a cheque for £50 and buried the notes in a glass jar in the garden. She buried a wooden box containing tinned food and a few bottles of wine in a separate place. Later she acquired an Anderson Shelter and erected it in a sandy pit some distance from the house. She and Helena spent two nights in it, when an 'Alert' had been sounded, but found it so uncomfortable that they preferred to be bombed in the house. A few months later, being short of a couple of pounds, Mother unearthed her money-jar, and then re-buried it in a different place.

No doubt all this would have confused an invading enemy; but a year later when the threat of invasion had lifted, we found it had confused Mother also. She searched for the money in vain. She simply could not remember where she had buried it. One weekend the whole family gathered at Heatherbrae to deal with the situation. Ted thought we might be able to mesmerise Mother, but he could not do it. I suggested that, subject to careful controls, we might lace her with whisky and lead her blindfolded round the garden in case she might have some water-divining sense. Again and again we searched, prodding the sand with walking sticks, but to no avail.

Some weeks later it was poor Cousin Daisy who, walking

in the garden, tripped and came down heavily on a very solid object, which turned out to be the elusive glass jar. When Mother delightedly pressed into her hand an unexpectedly large reward Cousin Daisy, who incidentally had also fallen on hard times, was overjoyed, and rather tactlessly praised *her* Guardian Angel for having so favoured her at Mother's expense.

'The Blitz.' Few that were then in London can forget it. In mid-September 1940, following the narrow defeat of the German Airforce in the Battle of Britain, Hitler reluctantly dispersed the massive invasion fleet that had gathered in every port and inlet along the French and Belgian coast, and concentrated the whole fury of his air attack on London. His purpose was to create such devastation and panic that the civil population would be driven to demand peace at any price. For sixty-seven nights in succession, as soon as darkness fell, the sirens sounded and waves of bombers were heard overhead, raining down thousands of incendiaries and hundreds of tons of high explosives. These included armour-piercing and delayed-action bombs, and area-devastation 'landmines'. This was a new type, floating down on a parachute and bursting above ground to produce a wider blast effect, making hundreds homeless. Even the children were not forgotten. For them there was the butterfly-bomb, a fascinating little contraption of coiled wires and wings which, when touched, blew them to pieces. There were also the daytime hit-and-run raids, to keep the sirens wailing and our nerves on edge. London was sorely stricken. In that year alone some 40,000 Londoners were killed or seriously injured, and a further 40,000 injured less seriously. But these figures of a year's casualties give little idea of the fearsome ordeal endured night after night by the millions who escaped physical injury.

Most of the seven million people remaining in the capital spent their nights dispersed in concrete shelters, or basements, or their individual family Anderson Shelters, which were at least splinter-proof. But as the bombing intensified and the number of homeless increased their thoughts turned naturally to the Tube stations. There on a cold rainy night they would find peace and warmth and a chance to sleep. But the London Passenger Transport Board, under their Chairman Lord Ashfield, had earlier taken a different view. They were strongly opposed to anything that might interfere with the free operation of the Underground Railways, which were so important to the life of the capital. They also knew the danger of crowds pressing down the stairways on to overcrowded platforms, and of people being pushed on to the live rail. If there was a disaster they would be blamed. So the Board's policy was, 'Regret, no shelterers.'

But when is a shelterer not a shelterer? Perhaps when he's a passenger. And the homeless and distressed Londoners were not to be denied. At first there were a few, paying minimum fares; soon many more, still paying; then in their thousands without payment they came. Not as yet a panicking mob (whatever Hitler's hopes may have been); always ready to go quietly where the station staff told them; with rolled-up blankets, with small tattered suitcases, with babies cradled in cardboard boxes, helping each other, in they came. They kept the way clear for peak-hour travellers, and were thankful for a night's respite even on a bed of concrete. At times the total number of shelterers approached 200,000 and the crowding and absence of sanitary arrangements on the platforms produced a situation that might have got out of hand before so very long. It was an awkward problem; and there was no sign that anyone was doing anything about it.

It so happened that, for my sins, I was at that time responsible for the operation of the London Transport canteen service, the largest industrial canteen service in the country. To put it briefly, we had 124 canteens situated all over London, ranging in size from Chiswick, which served 5,000 maintenance men, down to a little hut on Putney Common serving four busmen at a time. In total, we were serving 112,000 cooked meals daily to London Transport's 80,000 staff. Although not infrequently several canteens at a time were out of action — in fact ten were totally destroyed — we kept the service going throughout the war. The 1600 canteen staff, mostly women, achieved this by their devoted work under difficult conditions. The problem of caring for the crowds sheltering in the Tubes would be even more difficult, and I pitied the poor devil who might be landed with it.

One Sunday in early October I visited Mother at her home in Surrey. The clean crisp autumn air, the gorgeous colouring of the trees and the peacefulness of the village church were a healing tonic for a jaded Londoner. In the evening we could see in the distance the searchlights probing the night sky and the flashes of the bombs as they stoked up the fires. I told Mother what was happening over there, and the sad sights to be seen among the wreckage. 'Poor people, how awful!' she said. She wanted so much to help; but she was then seventy, and what could she do?

In her bedroom a small framed quotation caught my eye. It said:

I expect to pass through this world but once; any good thing therefore that I can do, or any kindness that I can show to any fellow-creature, let me do it now; let me not defer it or neglect it, for I shall not pass this way again.

That's not for me, I thought. There's more than enough on my plate already. Yet it rankled, and somehow would not go away.

A few days later something prompted me to see what was happening down below in the Tubes. The sirens had gone and in the darkness I parked my car in a little blind alley at Holborn Station and went inside. It was an astonishing sight. Every available space below ground level was covered with inert bodies. It was like the aftermath of a massacre. Where shortly before there had been the hustle and bustle of the rush hour, now there was neither sound nor movement. One or two, still awake, were ready to talk, softly not to wake the others. They told of finding their homes wrecked, friends or relations missing or gone away. Tomorrow the anxious search would continue for those buried in the rubble. Some had come down just for a night or two to relax in safety before returning to take up life on the surface once more.

Sometimes the story needed no words. I watched a young man intent on giving a baby its bottle. He was not very good at it, and was getting advice from two older women at his side. The family belongings were now contained in a shopping bag. He concentrated wholly on the baby as if to shut out for a while the horror which they had so recently survived. Stepping carefully over the recumbent forms on the platform, I saw that most of the children were sleeping as care-free as if in their own beds. But among the grown-ups not a few had the withdrawn expression that suggested they had frozen their feelings and were beyond tears. Yet here and there some gallant soul kept the Cockney humour going, so that for a little while they might forget what tomorrow would have in store. Reaching the platform edge, where a four-foot strip was kept clear for the movement of passengers, I boarded a train on the Piccadilly Line, and later took a trip on the Central Line. Everywhere it was the same; worn-out crowds asleep on the hard dirty floors, and nothing being done to comfort them. He would need to have a heart of stone who would not react strongly to that situation.

It was near midnight when I emerged into Kingsway and regained my car. The streets were pitch dark, except for a momentary glimmer as a searchlight's beam swung across the sky. But there was no lack of noise: there was the crashing of the barrage, the whine and thump of falling bombs, the clanging of fire-engines and ambulances as they raced through the empty streets. I went at a crawl up Southampton Row, crossed the Euston Road, and settled down to follow the dimmed-out rear-light of a north-bound tram-car. And all the way home the idea grew clearer and clearer in my head that somehow, at whatever cost, I must find some way to help those thousands of distressed people; and quickly, 'for I shall not pass this way again'.

By next morning the plan had taken shape. It is well known that for people of all ages who are shocked or distressed there is nothing like a cup of hot sweet tea. I realised too with some dismay that no one was better placed to get it to those thousands of shelterers than myself. I had the necessary large-scale catering experience. Above all I knew the departmental heads of London Transport, and many of the railway officials. It just had to be me.

Consider the problem. One could hardly find a place less suitable for serving tea, and perhaps other refreshments, than a Tube Station platform. There was neither running water nor drainage. Cooking was ruled out because of the limited ventilation, nor would it be safe to have a naked flame. The people packed on the platforms would have to be served without moving from their places, otherwise they might obstruct the passengers, and perhaps be pushed on to the live rail. Along with cups of tea, large quantities of biscuits and buns would be wanted, and hot pies too. How were these to be delivered daily, and cleared away daily, up and down lifts or staircases at more than seventy stations throughout the London area, with never a failure? Obviously we could not rely on the big tea-shop contractors. It must all be done by train, by ourselves, and quickly.

But that was easier said than done. It would be a totally new idea to London Transport. And we would have to find the answer to some technical problems before we could be sure the scheme would work. For instance, how does a train deliver goods along a line on which passenger trains are running every two minutes? Next, how to make tea on that huge scale? Until I could assure my Member on the London Transport Board that it could be done, we would not get approval to start. I telephoned the Sales Manager of a large electrical firm to ask if they could supply within ten days 200 ten-gallon electric laundry-boilers. They could. Armed with that promise, and a good deal of faith and hope, I launched the idea with my Board Member as a matter of urgency. He was non-committal, but would consider it. I heard nothing. Four days later the *Star* came out with the intriguing headline 'L.P.T.B. to feed in tubes'. This was promptly denied by 'London Transport spokesman'. Two days later a high official of the Ministry of Food came to see me, and asked if it could be done. I said it could, and it should.

On 25 October a meeting was held at the Ministry of Food. Lord Woolton, the Minister, silver-haired and charming, took the Chair with Lord Ashfield opposite him. Other Ministry officials and my Board Member were present. Lord Woolton opened by emphasising the anxiety of the Government over the morale of the shelterers. A few undesirables had already tried to work up some agitation to have the bombing stopped by negotiation! Therefore everything possible must be done to maintain morale — and there was nothing like a hot cup of tea! Lord Ashfield admitted that there might be a need, but his job was passenger transport and it was most undesirable that anything should be allowed to interfere with that. Catering for the public, he said, should be done by the large catering firms. Back came the answer: those firms had been consulted, but had declined to undertake it. So the discussion proceeded. Presently Lord Woolton's line became stronger and firmer. He really could not accept that it was beyond the powers of London Transport to provide some refreshments to the shelterers as a war-time measure only. There was an embarrassing pause. Suddenly Lord Ashfield turned on me and angrily demanded, 'Do you know what you're doing, Gordon?'

(There are moments when the brain works with the speed of lightning, even mine. Why, I thought, had our Chairman and my Board Member not yet had one word of discussion with me about the possibilities? Could it be because they didn't want to be involved? Then if the attempt should fail it would only be my head that rolled. Evidently there was to be no support from our Chairman. As to his question, it would be useless to answer truthfully, 'I hope so', or even, 'I think so'. For the sake of the shelterers then, I must take a chance, and to hell with the consequences.)

'Yes, sir,' I replied firmly. But I was not out of the wood yet.

'Well, what preparations have you made?'

'I've got an option on 200 large electric boilers for immediate delivery.'

The cross-examination ended there without further comment; but there was a rewarding smile from Lord Woolton. And so the scheme went into action, without instructions from the Board. They didn't say 'No'. They just remained aloof and waited. On my head be it.

Three days later we opened experimentally at Holland Park; and three days after that at Shepherd's Bush. Then followed the rest of the Central London Line, the Northern Line, the Bakerloo, the Piccadilly. Within six weeks of that meeting, those thousands of shelterers were being fed and refreshed night and morning from 129 tea-points at 71 stations underground. And, most important of all, there were smiles and jokes where previously there had been fears and despair. We can take it, they said.

On 16 November, *The Times* reported:

Vigorous cheering marked the progress of the first Tube Refreshment Special, the passengers on which included the Lord Mayor of London, and the Minister of Food, Lord Woolton. 'This is a magnificent piece of organisation,' he said. 'London Transport have jumped in in an emergency and done a job that has nothing really to do with them. I asked Lord Ashfield if he would use his organisation to see that the people had food night and morning. He replied that if I would provide the equipment he would do the rest.' Lord Ashfield was another passenger on the 'special', and so was Lord Horder who was specially interested in the first-aid station at Notting Hill Gate.

I personally only heard the cheering from a distance, not having been invited on this all-star special. I was in any case busy making arrangements for the Piccadilly Line. The other lines came later.

This is how it was done. Our own Building Superintendent piped a water-supply down from street level to each tea-point, as soon as I agreed it with the Station Master. Then the Signal Engineer's Assistant installed power cables for the tea-making boilers. That took in all 44 miles of electric cable. Then we got a firm to supply 800 fibre food-bins of special design, fitted with trays and padlocks, for the food had to be delivered to the platforms at a time when there was no one on duty to receive it. We also bought hundreds of food-baskets and 2-gallon long-spouted watering-cans, which we found to be the best means of serving food and drink to each shelterer in his or her own place. Drainage we had to ignore; we did no washing up, and shelterers were soon bringing their own mugs. Elsan closets were provided at platform level when the crowds thinned out a little and people could safely move around. The use of W.C.s and the pumping of sewage up to street-level came later.

It took time to assemble a new organisation of office staff for this new service. I told my assistants in the canteen organisation to carry on as far as possible without me; which they did disconcertingly well. My new organisation leaders were taken in part from other London Transport departments, and in part by outside advertisement.

Nearly 1,000 women helpers had to be recruited, medically examined, uniformed and paid, which was done by our existing organisation. The best of them were quickly promoted as Line and Section Supervisors.

The most challenging problem was how to get the supplies to the tea-points in the tunnels. We bought these supplies daily from a large catering firm. I insisted that they should be collected by our own vans, and delivered to our seven Railway Depots. The Operating Manager of the Underground Railways agreed to set aside seven special trains for our sole use, and supplied the train crews. As each driver changed duties weekly, one of our staff had to travel in the cab to tell him the exact location of the tea-point at the next stop, and which train door should draw up opposite it. This was important, for at each station we could only allow 20 seconds stop for delivering the supply bins and collecting the empties. Each train left the depot at a scheduled time to take its place in the normal train service. The train windows were placarded 'Tube Refreshments Special', 'No entry', with 'Stand Clear Please' on the sliding doors to discourage would-be passengers from entering. Each of our trains, known before long as 'the Bun Specials', ran as close as possible to the passenger train in front, and never were the passenger services delayed on our account. All this required most precise and conscientious work from many members of the staff in their various jobs. But they worked with a wonderful spirit. I had wall-posters displayed in each food-depot, saying, 'This Depot supplies X Stations, and feeds X shelterers. They rely on us for food and drink night and morning. We must not let them down.' They never did. It could easily have happened; a personal misunderstanding, a strike, a breakdown, someone's temper lost, someone absent without being covered. But they were kept fully informed and were not just working for the money. That brought out the best in everyone.

At the seven railway depots, the engineers achieved the

nearly impossible to help us. Whenever the surface tracks were cut by bombs it was they who found some other way to get the train safely into the tunnel. As long as they could keep things going, we didn't hear from them. What more could one ask? Additionally, lorries were available for delivery in case the power supply was cut; but they were rarely required.

This was our Menu, when electric hot-cupboards had been added to the original installation of wash-boilers:

HOT		COLD	
Tea and Cocoa	1d	Cheese Rolls	2d
Soup	1½d	Biscuits, pkt	2d
Meat Pie	4d	Buns and Cakes	1d
Cornish Pasty	3d	Chocolate Bar	2d
Sausage Roll	2d	Fresh Apple	1½d
Potato Crisps	2d		
Apple Turnover	3d	(Babies' Milk warmed free of charge)	

After a while the dietetic experts at the Ministry of Food became concerned lest the bombed-out Londoners were not getting enough vitamins owing to their restricted food supplies and the dislocation of vegetable and fruit markets. They hit on the idea of making good the deficiency through the Tube Refreshment Service. A Wonder-Soup was evolved. It contained many root vegetables and all the vitamins then known, and for good measure they laced it freely with yeast. It tasted good. But within an hour or two it became almost explosive. Queues rapidly formed outside every lavatory within walking distance. Protests followed. The experiment was never repeated.

The Public Health Authorities then came into the picture with fears that the Tube Shelters might be breeding-grounds for epidemics of colds, influenza, diphtheria and mosquito-borne infections. Plans were made to introduce disinfectant into the existing ventilation system. There was an experiment at Marble Arch, which made everyone cough and complain of sore throats. Thereafter the treatment was suspended. It is a strangely perverse fact that in spite of (or could it be because of?) all the hardships that Londoners had to endure during the Blitz winter of 1940–1, their health remained well above average.

By the end of 1941 the total figure of shelterers had fallen to 10,000 or 20,000 nightly. We maintained a minimum service in readiness, for two more years. Then in February 1944, flying bombs ('doodle-bugs') started coming over. The total of shelterers suddenly rose to 150,000, and we were back in business. But after several months the numbers gradually decreased until September 1944, when the flying bombs were superseded by 'rockets'. People then became more fatalistic. At last 'Tube Refreshments' was wound up on V.E. Day.

But to return now to November 1940. When the first Tube Refreshment Special rolled along the Central Line, and the venture was shown to be a success, congratulations and thanks came to me from the Ministry of Food. They told me, too, that the Prime Minister, who amid all his preoccupations had asked for a week-by-week report on the measures for helping the shelterers, was pleased at the way things had gone. And when I heard that, somehow the continuing silence of our Chairman mattered very little.

Mother, too, had read various accounts of these events in the papers. One passage in particular had touched her. It was from the *Daily Herald*:

> One regrets that there is no Dickens to write about it, no Hogarth to leave a biting and breath-catching picture for all time. Because here, below ground, is the tender sentimental side of London. Other cities might grant shelter, but not this care. London, like Jerusalem, gathers her children under her wing.

When I next went to see Mother, 'Well done,' she said,

'you have been much in my thoughts — and in my prayers.'

'Bless you,' I replied, 'I feared as much! But now that the worst is over, do please call off your Guardian Angel and his friends. They've fairly run me off my feet. All I want now is a rest!'

Mother smiled to herself and said nothing.

When the local Home Guard was formed Helena, who was doing hospital secretarial work, also became Company Clerk in a company commanded by Col. J. H. Mackenzie C.M.G., D.S.O., Colonel of the Royal Scots Regiment. Late in 1943 they both realised that their partnership was meant to last, so they were married and lived in Colonel Jack's house in the same village. At the end of the war, as his lease expired, they came to live with Mother at Heatherbrae. As Helena frankly said, 'Of course it was a difficult position. I had lived with her all my life, and there were naturally times when she would call me into her room to discuss family matters, while Jack thought I belonged to him and he had first call. With great understanding she thought this could not go on, and said she would try out a hotel at Eastbourne.'

Mother, with even greater economy of language, just recorded, 'It was then more suitable for me to retire from the scene.' That after more than fifty years of running our family home she should make over to Helena and Jack her house, its furnishings and contents, and begin hotel life in Eastbourne with few, if any, local friends at the age of seventy-four was to my view a decision of great courage and self-denial.

She must have looked back over the years with very mixed feelings. From the golden days of Monzievaird, when she had presided over a family of five and a staff of seven, she had perforce become used to living alone and doing the shopping, the cooking, much of the cleaning, a little gardening, and gathering and chopping of firewood, and the feeding and medical attention of half-a-dozen hens.

Mother accepted these changing social conditions of her time without complaint; but she was most reluctant to give up any of her activities on the score of age.

One day on Helena's monthly garage bill there appeared an item — 'To two driving lessons — £1. 5. 0.' Inquiries at first threw no light on the entry, which was considered to be an error by the garage. But when Helena challenged her directly about it Mother, reddening a little, confessed. Well, as a matter of fact, yes; she had wanted to see what it was like to drive; and the young man at the garage had been quite encouraging. But why two lessons? Well, you see, she had so very much wanted to see if she *could*. All sorts of incompetent people drove, and why couldn't she? It was only after two lessons that she had to admit that in an emergency her reactions might not be quite quick enough, and this might endanger someone else's life (never her own), which was a risk she had decided not to take. She had therefore resigned herself to travelling by bicycle.

At Eastbourne Mother found much in hotel life to make up for the loss of her home. Once more she was able to attend the Presbyterian services at St Andrew's Church, where she had worshipped as a girl. There she soon made friends. Relieved of all anxieties over housekeeping and housework, she was able to give her time and energies in other directions where they were needed. For a while she was a film-goer, but she found the continual emphasis on sex something of a bore. Not that she was easily shocked; for after watching a sample of Hollywood passion which faded out with the hero sprawled over the heroine, her only comment was, 'A little *suggestive*, don't you think?'

My daughter Ann, who was then at school at Eastbourne, tells of her visits to 'Grannie'. The girls went in a school party to St Andrew's Church, and she always noticed Grannie from her striking trilby-type hat of purple velour, still with a feather in it, contrasting gaily with her snow-white hair. They would lunch at the hotel and later have tea in her bedroom. Because war-time rationing was still in force, Grannie would have been saving some of her rations all the week in envelopes in her capacious handbag, with a jar of butter and a pot of jam in her wardrobe, and a few odd cakes from a sale of work. A little table-cloth would be spread over her box, and tea made at the basin with a portable electric saucepan. Then she would produce her private ornaments and albums of family photographs, and Ann would be entertained with endless stories of Grannie's family, and of the doings of her second son when he was a little boy.

In 1950 Mother, rejoicing in her independence, joined at short notice a coaching party on an eight-day tour to see the Passion Play at Oberammergau, 'which I found a wonderful experience, and am glad I lived to see it'. In the following year, she hatched up a scheme to join a cousin on a trip to South Africa, where she had a married son. However the cousin was 82 years of age and not too strong, and her other sons strongly dissuaded her from undertaking such a journey. 'But I, being two years younger and in good health, felt a strong urge to go because I had never been there before. And so with some helpful advice from the General Secretary of the Mission to Lepers, I set off on my adventures alone.'

Yet she was not really alone. She admitted that on finding her ship's cabin full of flowers she was 'quite overcome with such a display of love and affection'. And then there was her Guardian Angel, by now involved in whole-time duty. It would be quite wrong to think of this Angel as a delusion of old age. Right up to the very end there were no delusions about Mother. Throughout her life she believed that 'all things work together for good to them that love God'. Particularly in her later years when, as she put it, she lived in a suitcase, ready to go, she had an absolute faith that all would be well, and found that it worked. Fears and anxieties had fallen away. Growing older in body, she grew younger in spirit.

Nor did she take this matter of her Guardian Angel

too seriously. To him was credited the calmness of the sea, and her winnings of the Sweep Stake (Oh, Mother!) on the ship's daily run. Some of it she blew on two bottles of hock — half a glass for her to drink the health of her invisible benefactor, and the rest for others at her table. As she confided to her diary: 'So much to be thankful for. I shall be on the rampage next month, having the time of my life!' Let her diary speak again for her, in condensed form:

That momentous visit exceeded all my expectations; the delightful relaxation of the three weeks' trip by sea to Cape Town; the journey by bus and coach some 900 miles, sometimes over very rough roads to visit Leper colonies at Pretoria and in Swaziland; and still more fun, my first and unpremeditated aeroplane journey from Johannesburg to Livingstonia, 900 miles in three hours; that marvellous spectacle, the Victoria Falls by moonlight; their majestic beauty and splendour enhanced by the iridescent glory of a lunar rainbow. The following morning in the early hours, I was out in a midget aeroplane hedge-hopping over Rhodesia; seeing elephants, giraffes, zebras, impala, ostriches and many other animals in flight from the unwelcome noise in their sky as we skimmed the tree-tops; rather a hair-raising experience.

There was also a memorable weekend when I was asked by some missionaries to give a short address through an interpreter, to a native congregation of some four hundred people. The Africans being so obsessed by evil spirits, I was led to speak to them about the guidance of Angels, so often promised and exemplified in scripture. In the extempore prayers that followed my talk, some of the audience besought the Heavenly Father that the same Angelic protection should take me safely home, prayers which have been abundantly answered. It has greatly touched me to hear, three years later, from one of those missionaries that the people still remember me as 'The Lady the Angels took care of'.

In Swaziland she met Zalakwanda Zulu, a leper patient she had been personally supporting through the Leper

Mission. Both his legs had been reduced to stumps and he was totally blind, but still a radiant Christian. To him, she renewed her simple message: 'If ever you are tempted to lose hope or be frightened, just call on your Father and he will give you the faith and courage to go on.'

Mother was very faithful to her lepers. She had already served for twenty-four years on the Council of the Leper Mission. On her return from Africa until she was ninety she regularly journeyed by coach from Eastbourne to London to attend Council meetings. She would carry in her capacious handbag a sandwich lunch and a thermos of coffee, which she consumed either on a seat in Regent's Park or in Ted's consulting room, according to the weather. She was quietly proud of the fact that, even when she was ninety, bus conductors never offered to help her in boarding or alighting.

In her mid-eighties she entered a London nursing-home for a fairly simple operation. A few days later she developed pneumonia, and we began to fear for her. Antibiotics repelled the attack, but she was left with a cold abscess in her lung which had to be drained by suction through a large needle, possibly a frightening process. But when I was allowed in to see her, she was sitting up in bed with a triumphant look in her eye. Now she had shared in some of what her wounded son had been through at the hospital at Boulogne!

She recovered well, and returned to convalesce at Eastbourne. That process gave her the opportunity to take a course in book-binding, and a few months later I found her in an upper room adjoining St Andrew's Church where, with bubbling glue-pot and yards of cloth, she was engaged in rebinding all the Church's hymn-books to the number of some five hundred. She then turned to tapestry and produced an elaborate and beautiful cushion cover for the Minister.

Just before she was ninety, she was guided to move to a Hindhead hotel, within a few miles of Heatherbrae, where

Helena and Jack still lived; and near to Bracken House, the retirement home of Ted and his wife. At the hotel she had a bed-sitting room on the ground floor, as stairs were becoming a nuisance. Here she launched out once more into flower-drawings, which she produced to a professional standard, giving the money she earned to her lepers.

Her ninetieth birthday, celebrated quietly at Heatherbrae, was a great occasion. Her three children were there, Teddy, Huntly and Helena, each with wife or husband. To avoid making the party distractingly large, her grandchildren were represented by their latest photographs. Mother was dressed in blue, her white hair beautifully done, and an unwonted touch of make-up had been added (unnecessarily) to her cheeks. There was a feeling that her Marathon Race had been run, she had outdistanced all her Victorian competitors from Uncle George to Aunt Sophy, and was now ready to finish off with a Lap of Honour. For the best part of two more years she lived quietly and patiently, reading and writing, keeping in touch with her friends, and always happy to see her grandchildren. On her bedside table one saw the two things she valued most, her heavily-annotated Bible and her photograph of Father.

And so we come to Christmas 1962, late in her ninety-second year. In October Ted's wife had died of the fell disease, and Mother had arranged to spend Christmas Day with him so that he should not feel lonely. She was still an active walker, doing two or three miles a day; but on Christmas Eve snow had fallen, and she strayed into the Devil's Punch Bowl and lost her way. When at last she got back to the hotel she was quite exhausted and very cold.

On Christmas Day when she reached Teddy he noticed the swollen ankles and the shadow in her face, and persuaded her to have a week's rest. A Hindhead nursing home had a vacancy, so he and Helena saw her comfortably installed next day, and Ted left for Rye where he had an annual golf engagement. Helena telephoned to me in

THE LONG, LONG TRAIL

Hampshire saying that what Mother needed was a good rest and there was nothing more to be done.

Two days later the snow started to fall in earnest, and kept on for two days and more. Helena could not get her car out of the garage. The snow lay everywhere between two and three feet deep. She telephoned to the nursing-home and was told that Mother's condition was not too good; the home itself was cut off, and the roads impassable. Our Hampshire village too was isolated.

On 31 December Helena gallantly struggled a mile through knee-deep snow to the bus-route, and was lucky to find a bus that took her near the nursing-home. She found Mother barely awake. She told her that Teddy sent his love; Huntly too. There was a perceptible nod, and a smile — her last farewell to us.

It was clear that she was now reaching out to the welcoming hands for which she had waited so long. And soon, still smiling, she fell asleep.

Green pastures are before me,
    Which yet I have not seen;
Bright skies will soon be o'er me,
    Where the dark clouds have been.
My hope I cannot measure;
    My path to life is free;
My Saviour has my treasure,
    And He will walk with me.